AF558539

MY MOTHER INDIA

This edition published by Lector House in 2024

ISBN: 978-93-6138-773-9
Edition copyright © 2024 by Lector House LLP
All rights reserved under the International Copyright Conventions.

Every possible effort has been made to ensure that the information contained in this book is accurate at the time of going to press and the publisher cannot accept responsibility for any errors or omissions, however caused, in this unabridged, slightly corrected republication of the text of the first edition. No responsibility for loss or damage occasioned to any person, acting or refraining from action, as a result of the material in this publication can be accepted by the publisher. The publisher is not associated with any product or vendor mentioned in the book. The contents of this work are intended to further general scientific research, understanding and discussion, only. Readers should consult with a specialist, where appropriate.

No part of this publication may be reproduced, stored in a retrieval system, or transmitted, in any form, or by any means, electronic, mechanical, photocopying or otherwise, without the prior permission of the publisher.

Lector House LLP
Registered Office: H. No. 96, Block C, Tomar Colony,
Burari, Delhi – 110084, India
info@lectorhouse.com
www.lectorhouse.com

MY MOTHER INDIA

DALIP SINGH SAUND

2024

LECTOR HOUSE LLP

MY MOTHER INDIA

BY

DALIP SINGH SAUND, M.A., PH.D.

Dedicated to
my beloved friend Dr. Bhagat Singh Thind

PREFACE

This work was undertaken at the request of THE PACIFIC COAST KHALSA DIWAN SOCIETY, commonly known as the SIKH TEMPLE at Stockton, California. The original plan was to write a comprehensive reply to Katherine Mayo's book MOTHER INDIA, which was changed later to one of producing a handbook on India for general use by the American public. In view of the momentous changes of worldwide interest, which have taken place in India during recent years, the need for such a book was quite imminent. And it was only fitting that THE PACIFIC COAST KHALSA DIWAN SOCIETY, in its role as the interpreter of Hindu culture and civilization to America, should undertake its publication.

Only a few years ago, India, like other countries of the Orient, was a far Eastern problem. To-day, if rightly judged, it has already become a near Western issue. Except for the few scholars of oriental history and literature, who occupied themselves diligently in exploring the hidden treasures of Hindu civilization, the name of India was an unknown thing to the rest of the American world. For the average man and woman in the United States the affairs of that oriental country were too remote an issue for them to notice. With the advances made by science during recent times, however, different parts of the world have become so near together, and their business and cultural relations have grown so desperately interlaced, that the affairs of one section of the globe cannot, and should not, remain a matter of comfortable unconcern for the other. It has been my aim in the preparation of this book to answer the various questions that commonly arise in the minds of the American people regarding the cultural and political problems of India. And if I have succeeded in bringing about a better understanding of India by the people of America, I consider myself amply repaid.

Wherever feasible I have made free uses of striking passages and phrases from the writings of several authors. Since these were copied from my notes gathered during a course of study extending over several years, it has not always been possible for me to trace the source, for which I wish to be humbly excused.

I wish to express my sincerest appreciation to my beloved wife for her untiring assistance in the preparation of the manuscript and the reading of the proofs. I wish also to thank my friend Mr. Anoop Singh Dhillon for valuable suggestions.

Los Angeles, California.
March, 1930.

DALIP SINGH SAUND.

CONTENTS

CHAPTER I

WOMAN'S POSITION IN INDIA. IS SHE BOND OR FREE?

"Where women are honored,
there the gods are pleased;
but where they are dishonored,
no sacred rite yields reward."

Thus, in the year 200 B. C., wrote Manu, the great law-giver of India—India, whose mind was full grown when the western nations were yet unborn; India, whose life rolled on while the West, like the dragon fly, lived and died to live again. While Europe was still in a state of primitive barbarism, the Indo-Aryans of *Bharat* (India) had reached an elevated state of moral and spiritual perfection; and in the realm of intellectual culture they had attained an eminence which has not yet been equalled by the most advanced of western countries. Not only had they a perfect alphabet and a symmetrical language, but their literature already contained models of true poetry and remarkable treatises on philosophy, science, and ethics when the forefathers of the modern western nations were still clothed in skins and could neither read nor write. In their firm grasp of the fundamental meaning and purpose of life, and in the organization of their society with a view to the full attainment of the fruits of life, namely, "to take from each according to his capacity, and to give to each according to his needs," they had attained to a high degree of excellence, which has been recognized by the greatest of both western and oriental scholars. Says Max Müller, the noted scholar of oriental languages:

> "If I were to look over the whole world to find out the country most richly endowed with all the wealth, power, and beauty that nature can bestow—in some parts a very paradise on earth—I should point to India. If I were asked under what sky the human mind has most fully developed some of its choicest gifts, has most deeply pondered on the greatest problems of life, and has found solutions of some of them which well deserve the attention even of those who have studied Plato and Kant—I should point to India. And if I were to ask myself from what literature we, here in Europe, we who have been nurtured almost exclusively on the thoughts of Greeks and Romans, and of one Semitic race, the Jewish, may draw that corrective which is most wanted in order to

make our inner life more perfect, more comprehensive, more universal, in fact more truly human, a life not for this life only, but a transfigured and eternal life—again I should point to India."[1]

Further, of the culture of this ancient people of India Sir Monier-Williams, sometime Boden Professor of Sanskrit in the University of Oxford, famous translator of Sanskrit drama, and author of many works on history and literature, speaks from an intimate knowledge of India derived from long residence in the country when he writes:

> "Indeed, I am deeply convinced that the more we learn about the ideas, feelings, drift of thought, religious and intellectual development, eccentricities, and even errors of the people of India, the less ready shall we be to judge them by our own conventional European standards—the less disposed to regard ourselves as the sole depositories of all the true knowledge, learning, virtue and refinements of civilized life—the less prone to despise as an ignorant and inferior race the men who compiled the laws of Manu, one of the remarkable productions of the world—who composed systems of ethics worthy of Christianity—who imagined the *Ramayna* and *Mahabharata,* poems in some respects outrivalling the Iliad and the Odyssey—who invented for themselves the sciences of grammar, arithmetic, astronomy, logic, and six most subtle systems of philosophy. Above all, the less inclined shall we be to stigmatize as benighted heathen the authors of two religions, however false, which are at this moment professed by about half the human race."[2]

Such a civilization has built up the enormous literature of the Hindus embodied in the *Vedas, Upnishads,* the epic poems of *Ramayna* and *Mahabharata,* and the immortal works of Kalidasa, a literature comprising in itself an achievement of the human mind which may be considered sublime, and of which any civilization, ancient or modern, may feel justly proud. The poetical merit of Kalidasa's *Sakuntala* is universally admitted, and it ranks among the best of the world's masterpieces of dramatic art. Its beauty of thought and its tenderness in the expression of feeling are exquisite, while its creative fancy is rich, and the charm of its spirit is full. Says Goethe:

> *"Wouldst thou the life's young blossoms and the fruits of its decline,*
> *All by which the soul is pleased, enraptured, feasted, fed,—*
> *Wouldst thou the earth and heaven itself in one sweet name combine?*
> *I name thee, O* Sakuntala, *and all at once is said."*

The epic poems of *Ramayna* and *Mahabharata* consist of stories and legends which form a splendid superstructure on the teachings contained in the earlier scriptures of the *Vedas*. By relating what the men and women of those times thought, said, and did, these poems illustrate in a highly instructive manner the general character and culture of the early Hindus. The stories contained in these

[1] Max Müller—*What India Can Teach Us.*

[2] Sir Monier-Williams—*Modern India and the Indians,* page 353.

poems, which, in fact, rival the best known epic poems of the world, tell us of the thoughts and beliefs, hopes and fears, joys and sorrows of the people of this earliest recorded period. Through these stories we learn the fundamental concepts which governed the religious and social life of the early Hindus; in them are revealed also the basic moral and spiritual laws which controlled the actions, "not only of gods and supernatural men, but of ordinary men and women of India." "They explain—by showing the degrees of danger incurred by such vices as anger and pride, deception and faithlessness, intemperance and impiety—the evil consequences of moral transgressions from both man-made and supernatural laws; and at the same time they emphasize the beauty of such virtues as patience and self-control, truthfulness and purity, obedience and filial love."[3]

As an illustration of the fascinating and elevated nature of its lofty idealism, we shall quote two passages from *Ramayna*. In the first, Rama, the ideal king, has determined to execute the will of his late father by staying in the forests as an exile for fourteen years. Sita, his wife and the heroine of the story, begs her lord and husband to allow her to accompany him in his exile to the forests and offers a picture highly expressive of pious conjugal love. Sita says:

> *"Thou art my king, my guide, my only refuge, my divinity.*
> *It is my fixed resolve to follow thee. If thou must wander forth*
> *Through thorny trackless forests, I will go before thee, treading down*
> *The prickly brambles to make smooth thy path. Walking before thee, I*
> *Shall feel no weariness: the forest thorns will seem like silken robes;*
> *The bed of leaves, a couch of down. To me the shelter of thy presence*
> *Is better far than stately palaces, and paradise itself.*
> *Protected by thy arm, gods, demons, men shall have no power to harm me.*
> *Roaming with thee in desert wastes, a thousand years will be a day;*
> *Dwelling with thee, e'en hell itself would be to me a heaven of bliss."*

In the second selection Rama is heard answering to the entreaties of Bharata, who has tried in vain to dissuade him from carrying out his design. The following is Rama's answer to the messenger of Bharata:

> "The words which you have addressed to me, though they recommend what *seems* to be right and salutary, advise, in fact, the contrary. The sinful transgressor, who lives according to the rules of heretical systems, obtains no esteem from good men. It is good conduct that marks a man to be noble or ignoble, heroic or a pretender to manliness, pure or impure. Truth and mercy are immemorial characteristics of a king's conduct. Hence royal rule is in its essence *truth*. On truth the world is based. Both sages and gods have esteemed truth. The man who speaks truth in this world attains the highest imperishable state. Men shrink with fear and horror from a liar as from a serpent. In this world the chief element in virtue is truth; it is called the basis of everything. Truth is lord in the world; virtue always rests on truth. All things are founded on truth; nothing is higher than it. Why, then, should

[3] Oman—*The Great Indian Epics.*

> I not be true to my promise, and faithfully observe the truthful injunction given by my father? Neither through covetousness, nor delusion, nor ignorance, will I, overpowered by darkness, break through the barrier of truth, but remain true to my promise to my father. How shall I, having promised to him that I would thus reside in the forests, transgress his injunction, and do what Bharata recommends?"

In *Mahabharata* again we find proof of the high esteem in which the manly virtues of truthfulness, charity, benevolence, and chivalry towards women were held by the ancient Hindus. The most important incident in the drama (Mahabharata), namely, the death of Bhishma, occurred when this brave and virtuous man, in fidelity to his pledge never to hurt a woman, refused to fight, and was killed by a soldier dressed in a woman's garb.

The drama is full of moral maxims, around each one of which the poet has woven a story in a beautiful and elegant manner.

> "If Truth and a hundred horse sacrifice were weighed together, Truth would weigh the heavier. There is no virtue equal to Truth, and no sin greater than falsehood."
>
> "For the weak as well as for the strong, forgiveness is an ornament."
>
> "A person should never do to others what he does not like others to do to him, knowing how painful it is to himself."
>
> "The man who fails to protect his wife earns great infamy here, and goes to hell afterwards."

"A wife is half the man, his truest friend;
A loving wife is a perpetual spring
Of virtue, pleasure, wealth; a faithful wife
Is his best aid in seeking heavenly bliss;
A sweetly-speaking wife is a companion
In solitude, a father in advice,
A mother in all seasons of distress,
A rest in passing through life's wilderness."

These great epic poems have a special claim to our attention because they not only illustrate the genius of a most interesting people, but they are to this day believed as entirely and literally true by the vast population of India. "Huge congregations of devout men and women listen day after day with eager attention to recitations of these old national stories with their striking incidents of moral uplift and inspiration; and a large portion of the people of India order their lives upon the models supplied by those venerable epics."

The subjection of woman was accepted as a natural thing by the entire West until very recent times. Woman was held in the eyes of the law as no better than a slave, and she was considered useful in society merely to serve and gratify man, her master. Truly, such a condition forms a dark page in the history of the race.

Mrs. Carrie Chapman Catt, in her foreword to Mill's *Subjection of Women*, writes:

> "In defense of these expressions [subjection and slavery used in Mill's essay] and the general character of the essay, it must be said that the position of women in society at that time [1869] was comparable to that of no other class except the slave. As the slave took the name of his master so the woman upon marriage gave up her own and took that of her husband. Like the slave, the married woman was permitted to own no property; as, upon marriage, her property real and personal, and all she acquired subsequently by gift, will, or her own labour, was absolutely in her husband's control and subject to his debts. He could even will away her marriage portion and leave her destitute. The earnings of the slave belonged to the master, those of the wife to the husband. Neither slave nor wife could make a legal contract, sue or be sued, establish business, testify in court, nor sign a paper as a witness. Both were said to be 'dead in law'.
>
> "The children of the slave belonged to the master; those of the wife to the husband. Not even after the death of the husband was the wife a legal guardian of her own children, unless he made her so by will. While living he could give them away, and at death could will them as he pleased. He dictated the form of education and religion that they should be taught, and if the parents differed in religion, the wife was forced to teach the husband's faith. Like the slave, if the wife left her husband she could take nothing with her, as she had no legal claim to her children, her clothing, nor her most personal possessions.
>
> "The law in many lands gave husbands the right to whip their wives and administer other punishments for disobedience, provided they kept within certain legal restrictions. Within the memory of those living in Mill's day, wife-beating was a common offense in England and America, husbands contending that they were well within their 'rights', when so doing.
>
> " ... Education, always considered the most certain sign of individual advancement, was either forbidden or disapproved, for women. No colleges and few high schools, except in the United States, were open to women. Common schools were less usual for girls than for boys and the number of totally illiterate women vastly exceeded the number of illiterate men. Religion was recommended to women as a natural solace and avenue of usefulness, but they were not permitted to preach, teach, or pray in most churches, and in many singing was likewise barred! The professions and more skilled trades were closed to them."

That such a state of things was ever tolerated in the advanced countries of Europe and America seems to us of India incredible. But it is, nevertheless, true.

As in the case of other social laws, the subjection of woman was the result of the fundamental ideals (or the lack of ideals) which governed the western society of those times. Men were still in that low state of development in which "Might was Right," and in which the law of superior strength was the rule of life. No pretension was made to regulate the affairs of society according to any moral law. The physical law which sanctioned traffic in human slaves, at the same time sustained the bondage of the weaker sex.

We now live in an age where the law of the strongest, in principle at least, has been abandoned as the guiding maxim of life. It is still very widely practised in individual as well as in national relationships, but always under the guise of higher social and cultural ends. The law of force as the avowed rule of general conduct has given place to ideals of social equality, human brotherhood, and international goodwill. How far such ideals are being actively followed by the different peoples of the world remains to be determined; but their profession as the symbol of good culture, at least, is universal.

The emancipation of woman in the West is thus a very recent achievement. Yet it is rightly considered by most thinkers the greatest single step forward in the advancement of the human race. Its tremendous importance in the future development of the race is realized now by all classes of people over the entire world. In fact, the social status of woman in any society is regarded by most people, and properly so, as the test of its civilization.

Through what hardships and dangers, privations and humiliations ran the thorny and uphill path of the early leaders of the women's suffrage movement. The deeds of true nobility and heroic determination that were performed by the pioneers of women's emancipation are very little known to the average man and woman of the present day. How numerous and difficult were the obstacles placed in the way of these pioneers by their brow-beating opponents, how bitter was the nature of their persecutions, how mean and foul the character of the insults offered them, and blind and obstinate the attitude of the governing class to their simple demand for justice are little realized by those who enjoy the legacy left by those liberators.

The high idealism which inspired the movement of the militant suffragettes in England is manifest in their every word and action. Their methods of peaceful, silent, dignified, conscious and courageous suffering, contrasted with the treacherous, cowardly, shameful, unmanly, and brutal attacks of their opponents, have received considerations of high merit from all sections of honest and fair-minded men the world over. Virtuous women belonging to the highest stations in life and possessing qualities of rare courage, purity, and self-denial were attacked in the most cowardly fashion by bands of strong-bodied hooligans, "felled to the ground, struck in the face, frog-marched, and tossed hither and thither in a shameless manner." "The women speakers were assaulted with dead mice and flocks of live mice, and flights of sparrows were let loose into their meetings. Paid gangs of drunken men were dispatched to the women's gatherings to sing obscene songs, and drown the voices of the speakers with the rattle of tin cans and the ringing of bells. Bands of suffragettes were attacked, struck down unconscious, and driven out over wet roads covered with carbide by gangs of Liberal volunteers. Suffragette leaders were imprisoned in the jails of England in groups of hundreds at a time and were meted out the fancy punishment of forcible feeding through a tube inserted into the stomach, a process which causes intense and lingering pain."[4] This barbarous treatment excited at once the horror and indignation of the whole civilized world. Yet all these brutalities were carried on under the very nose, in fact, at the direction of the full-fledged Liberal members of the British cabinet.

At a campaign meeting held in Swansea where the suffragettes attempted to ask Mr. Lloyd-George questions regarding his attitude on the problem of woman franchise, he is reported as having used such language as, "sorry specimens of womanhood," "I think a gag ought to be tried," "By and by we shall have to order sacks for them, and the first to interrupt shall disappear," "fling them ruthlessly out," and, "frog-march them." At another meeting held in Manchester, February 4th, 1906, where Mr. Winston Churchill spoke, on asking a very simple question, the fourteen year old daughter of Mrs. Pankhurst, Adela, was savagely attacked, thrown down, and kicked by several men.

The unwholesome and bitter experiences of the peaceful and gentle suffragettes at the two election campaigns in May, 1907, are described by Miss Sylvie E. Pankhurst as follows:

> "After these stormy meetings the police and hosts of sympathisers always escorted us home to protect us from the rowdies. Just as we reached our door there was generally a little scuffle with a band of youths who waited there to pelt us with sand and gravel as we passed.... At Uppingham, the second largest town, the hostile element was smaller than at Oakham, but its methods were more dangerous. While Mary Gawthorpe was holding an open-air meeting there one evening, a crowd of noisy youths began to throw up peppermint 'bull's eyes' and other hard-boiled sweets. 'Sweets to the sweet,' said little Mary, smiling, and continued her argument, but a pot-egg, thrown from the crowd behind, struck her on the head and she fell unconscious...."

This is what happened on October 16th, 1909, at an open-air gathering near Dundee, where Mr. Winston Churchill was to speak:

> " ... Standing in the road were some thirty or forty men, all wearing the yellow rosettes of official Liberal stewards, and as the car (containing four prominent suffragettes) slowed, they rushed furiously towards it, shouting and tearing up sods from the road and pelting the women with them. One man pulled out a knife and began to cut the tires, whilst the others feverishly pulled the loose pieces off with their fingers. The suffragettes tried to quiet them with a few words of explanation, but their only reply was to pull the hood of the motor over the women's heads and then to beat it and batter it until it was broken in several places. Then

[4] E. Sylvie Pankhurst.

> they tore at the women's clothes and tried to pull them out of the car, whilst the son of the gentleman in whose ground the meeting was being held drove up in another motor and threw a shower of pepper in the women's eyes.... The only excuse for the stewards who took part in this extraordinary occurrence is that many of them were intoxicated."[5]

And the most pitiful part of the business was that such conduct seemed to be regarded by its perpetrators as engaging pieces of gallantry.

While a recitation of these incidents might be continued indefinitely, one more will suffice to show with what contempt and dishonor the western world has treated its women. On August 2, 1909, a great Liberal fete was held at Canford Park, near Poole in Dorsetshire. There were sports and games and Mr. Churchill was to deliver an address on the budget. Annie Kenney with three companions attended the fete, and the story of what took place is best told in her own words. She says:

> "As we entered the Park together we saw two very young girls being dragged about by a crowd of Liberal men, some of whom were old enough to be their fathers. They had thrown a pig net over them, and had pulled down their hair. We heard afterward that these girls came from a village near by, but the Liberals suspected them to be Suffragettes and ordered them out of the Park. ..., but they were crowded round us and the language they used is not fit for print.... They were calling out to each other to get hold of me and throw me into the pond which was very near ..., but as soon as my back was turned they started dragging me about in a most shameful way. One man who was wearing the Liberal colours pulled a knife out of his pocket, and to the delight of the other staunch Liberals, started cutting my coat. They cut it into shreds right from the neck downwards. Then they lifted up my coat and started to cut my frock and one of them lifted up my frock and cut my petticoat. This caused great excitement. A cry came from those Liberals, who are supposed to have high ideas in public life, to undress me. They took off my hat and pulled down my hair, but I turned round upon them and said that it would be their shame and not mine. They stopped then for a minute, and then two men, also wearing the Liberal colours, got hold of me and lifted me up and afterwards dragged me along, not giving me an opportunity to walk out in a decent way."[6]

The heroism and rare genius of Mrs. E. Pankhurst and her associates in the suffragette movement will be acknowledged by their friends and foes alike. Through their sufferings they have bequeathed to women of the western world the priceless heritage of Freedom, and thus pushed the progress of the human race a long step forward. Mrs. Pankhurst possessed, undoubtedly, a firm character, a lofty mind, a generous heart, strong and vigorous good sense. We shall call the emancipator of

[5] E. Sylvie Pankhurst—*The Suffragette,* page 451.
[6] E. Sylvie Pankhurst—*The Suffragette,* page 413.

English womanhood a great woman, using that word not as a cheap, unmeaning title but as conveying three essential elements of greatness, namely, unselfishness, honesty, and boldness. She who sacrificed everything for the voice of justice and submitted herself and her three young daughters to cruel indignities and hardships of jail life for the sake of her fellow creatures was an unselfish, an honest, a bold woman,—was a great woman—in the best sense of the word. And at this distant time as a proof of our honest affection and admiration for her goodness and virtue, we can afford to express a feeling of mingled sorrow and joy at her prolonged sufferings and final success.

In India, on the contrary, in the development of their wonderful civilization men and women have played an equal part. The two sexes have worked side by side in every branch of their spiritual endeavor, and women have attained the same eminence as men in higher learning. The Vedic hymns mention both men and women as divine revealers of Truth and as spiritual instructors of mankind. In fact, The Rig Veda, the earliest scriptural record of the world, contains hymns revealed by women; and the Hindu god, Indra, is described as being initiated into the knowledge of the Universal Spirit by the woman Aditi. Furthermore, the Upnishads, the philosophical portion of the Veda, frequently mention the names of women who discoursed on philosophical topics with the most learned men philosophers of the times. Women scholars were often appointed arbitrators and umpires in important philosophic debates, and the names of the two women philosophers, Gargi and Maitreyi, are familiar to all students of Hindu philosophy. In other words, the paths of intellectual culture were equally open to men and women, under exactly similar circumstances. In fact, the very spirit of such equality is inculcated in the minds of the people from both their law and their religion that made no distinction between the sexes in the award of honors for merit. The law-givers of India, taking their lessons from the Vedas, established the fundamental equality of man and woman by defining the relation of the sexes thus:

> "Before the creation of this phenomenal universe, the first born Lord of all creatures divided his own self into two halves, so that one half should be male and the other half female."

Not only in the direction of scholarly pursuits, but in the practical business affairs of the world also, the women of India have distinguished themselves eminently as legislators, ministers, commercial leaders, and military commanders. Men, women, and children throughout India are familiar with the story of Queen Chand Bibi, who defended Ahmedanagar during the long siege by the Grand Moghul; poets also have sung of her valor and administrative wisdom. Another instance of the recognition of the ability of women is the story of Nur Jahan (Light of the Universe), the beautiful queen of the Moghul Emperor, Jahangir, who guided the affairs of her husband's vast territories in a highly efficient manner for a period of nearly ten years. Further, and well known to all students of history, is the story of Mumtaz-i-Mahal, Emperor Shah Jahan's consort, who assisted him in his works of administration and in the construction of the famous buildings of his period. This woman, described as a person of unexampled dignity, delicacy, and charm, during her life-time was the "light of his eyes," and after death the perpet ual source of inspiration to the bereaved Emperor. On her death-bed, Mumtaz, the beloved companion of his life's happy days and mother of his six children, asked of Shah Jahan that a memorial befitting a queen be placed over her grave. In compliance with this request, and as a token of his unceasing love for the deceased queen, the Emperor constructed on her grave the famous Taj Mahal—a monument which by its beauty has made immortal the love it commemorates. The most beautiful building in the world stands as a memorial to man's love for his wife—an unconquerable love, unbroken and unsatisfied. Says Sir Edwin Arnold:

> "He has immortalised—if he could not preserve alive for one brief day—his peerless wife.... Admiration, delight, astonishment blent in the absorbed thought with a feeling that human affection never struggled more ardently, passionately and triumphantly against the Oblivion of Death. There is one sustained, harmonious, majestic sorrowfulness of pride in it, from the verse on the entrance which says that 'the pure of heart shall enter the Gardens of God', to the small, delicate letters of sculptured Arabic upon the tombstone which tell, with a refined humility, that Mumtaz-i-Mahal, the 'Exalted of the Palace', lies here, and that 'Allah alone is powerful.'"[7]

The heroic command of her own forces by the Rani (Queen) of Jhansi during the Indian War of Independence in 1857 is a familiar and more recent example of a woman entering into practical affairs. Clad in a man's uniform, she rode at the head of her troops, and died a brave and patriotic death in the battlefield. The name of Rani Jhansi is mentioned among the renowned heroes of the country, and as a special tribute to her loving memory her picture in a general's uniform is kept in many homes. Indian society is not opposed to the active participation of its women in the higher affairs of their national life. If the positive declarations of a group of western critics to the contrary were true, the action of Rani Jhansi would be condemned instead of being so universally applauded as it is now by even the most orthodox of old Hindu ladies.

Throughout the long history of India, then, women have not been hampered by any man-made restrictions from serving in the country's religious life, from fighting on its battlefields, and from holding power in its councils. In the present generation we find women again taking an active and important part in the affairs of the country. They have the fullest freedom for self-expression, of which they seem to have availed themselves in a highly creditable and fitting manner, without sacrificing the admiration and respect of the men. In times of their country's need they have given proofs of patriotism by self-sacrifice which speaks the language of love and devotion to motherland. With a voluntary desire to coöperate, the men of India have given to the women of the country a large share in its councils, and have invited them to their national conferences of importance. In the inner and more weighty deliberations of its leaders their influence is evident, and on all occasions of national demonstration the women of India are represented.

Shrimati Lajiavati—a frail, delicate figure, but a beautiful model of womanly

[7] Sir Edwin Arnold—*India Revisited,* page 211.

courage and dignity—has won for herself in the Punjab a place which is closely akin to worship. She founded, and is now managing as its principal, the Arya Samaj Kanya Mahavidyala (girls' school) in Jallundhar City, Punjab. Another example of India's modern women, who stands high in her countrymen's esteem, is Shrimati Ramabai Ranade. Her work as the secretary of Seva Sadhan, a society for social service work among the women of the country, has been amply recognized. During the debate over the women's suffrage bill in the Bombay Legislative Council, one honorable member remarked amid the greatest applause of the season: "There is no Council which would not be honored, graced, and helped by the presence of such a woman as one who is known to us all, Mrs. Ramabai Ranade." Mrs. Margaret E. Cousins, describing her interview with Mrs. Ranade, says:

> "I asked her, 'What do you think of the future of women in India?' 'It is full of hope and promise', she replied, and in doing so spontaneously took my hand and pressed it. It touches a Westerner when her Eastern sister does that. It bridges gulfs and knits the human sisterhood together. Like Mirabai of the poet's intuition she
>
> *Wears little hands*
> *Such as God makes to hold big destinies.*
>
> "Her hands revealed her soul, for in their touch was soft sweetness and strong vitality which still inspire me, and which promise the blessing of her remarkable powers of service to humanity for years to come."[8]

Where is the Indian whose heart does not beat with joy at the mention of Mrs. Sarojini Naidu? Who does not remember with feelings of proud exultation the name of this beloved and revered sister—she who is the symbol of patriotism and a flower of womanly beauty and culture, from whose elevated soul radiate grace, charm, and affection, and who is the object of her countrymen's adoration? In 1925, in recognition of her manifold virtues, the people of India exalted her to the highest position at their command; she was unanimously elected President of the Indian National Congress.[9] *In the entire history of mankind no woman has been more highly honored by her countrymen than has Mrs. Sarojini Naidu.* Read her poems and you will find the heart of a woman forever seeking the satisfaction of hungry love:

> *"Hide me in a shrine of roses,*
> *Drown me in a wine of roses,*
> *Drawn from every fragrant grove!"*

Listen to her musical eloquence on the nationalist platform of India, and you will hear the cry of a patriot's heart groaning under the load of its country's humiliation from the merciless foreign yoke.

> "Our arts have degenerated, our literatures are dead, our

[8] Margaret E. Cousins—*The Awakening of Asian Womanhood*, page 114.

[9] The Indian National Congress is the largest representative body of the Indian nation, with its ramifications spread throughout the country consisting of thousands of branches. Its meetings are held annually in different parts of the country.

> beautiful industries have perished, our valor is done, our fires are dim, our soul is sinking."

A more striking proof of the confidence and respect which the men of India bear towards their women was given during the debates on women's suffrage bills in the provincial legislative councils of the country. The Southborough Franchise Committee, which was formed to study the general conditions in the country with a view to granting the franchise to the people of India, in its report to the British Government of India (1919) had expressed its decision against granting the franchise to Indian women. This decision was upheld by the British Government of India in the statement, "In the present conditions of India we agree with them [the Southborough Committee] that it is not practical to open the franchise to women." To this decision of the Government Sir C. Sankaran Nair, the Indian member of the Executive Council, entered a strong protest, based on the strength of the evidence which was presented before the Southborough Committee in favor of granting franchise to women. His contention, furthermore, was upheld by the resolution passed at two successive sessions of the Indian National Congress (Calcutta 1917 and Delhi 1918). This resolution expressed in an unequivocal manner the opinion of the Indian nation on the important question of woman franchise as follows:

> "Women possessing the same qualifications as are laid down in any part of the [Reform] Scheme shall not be disqualified on account of sex."

A tremendous agitation was staged in India after the publication of the dispatch of the Government of India, unfavorable to women's rights. As a result of this agitation a provision was made whereby the provincial legislatures were given the power to admit or exclude women from franchise at their individual options. True to their traditions and following the teaching of their ancient as well as their modern seers the majority of the provinces have already granted the franchise to women on the same basis as to men. This experience is unequalled in the entire history of mankind. Everywhere else where the women enjoy any rights to vote or possess property, they have had to fight a battle involving prolonged hardships and outrageous indignities imposed upon them by the indignant and oftentimes barbarous ruling sex. India is the only civilized country of the world in which women in modern times have been granted franchise on an equality with men without a single demonstration of insult or disrespect directed against its aspiring womanhood. If for no other reason, the respect which the people of India have shown to the desire of their women for the franchise, should entitle them to a high place in the scale of civilization.

Mrs. Margaret E. Cousins is an international figure in the woman's suffrage movement, in which cause she has suffered imprisonments in both Ireland and England. She is also the founder and Honorary Secretary of the Women's Indian Association with its fifty branches spread over the country, and has lived for twelve years among the women of India with relations of intimate friendship. Mrs. Cousins is not in any sense of the word addicted to indiscriminate flattery, but she says:

> "Turning then to India one finds that though the percentage of education is appallingly low, the tradition of Indian law leaves women very free to take any position for which they show themselves capable. No Indian political organisations were at any time closed to women. Women have at every stage of Indian history taken high positions in their country's public service. Springing from their religious philosophy there is fundamentally a belief in sex equality, and this shows itself when critical periods demand it. This has been clearly shown during the movement of the past ten years for self-government. Women have had their share in all the local Conferences and in the National Congress. No one who was present can easily forget the sight of the platform at the Calcutta Congress of 1917 when three women leaders, Mrs. Annie Besant, President of the Congress, Mrs. Sarojini Naidu, representative of the Hindu women, and Bibi Ammam, mother of the Ali brothers and representative of the Muslim women, sat side by side, peeresses of such men leaders (also present) as Tilak, Gandhi and Tagore, and receiving equal honor with them."[10]

As a distinct contribution towards the solution of the world's social problems, the *East Indians*, by allowing woman the exercise of her own free will and the entire responsibility of all her actions, have established the fact that a woman left completely to herself with opportunity to develop freely her instincts and faculties, may equal man in reason, wisdom, and uprightness, and may surpass him in delicacy and dignity.

The Hindu religion has always stood for the absolute equality of woman with man. In matters religious as well as secular the Hindu woman has been considered the equal of man before the law since the origin of the Hindu nation. The admission of women into American universities began only in recent times, while her partial equality in the sight of law, not yet quite complete, is less than twenty years old. But in India women have enjoyed such rights and many more since the beginning of its recorded history. To the western readers who have been very injudiciously fed upon missionaries' tales about India, with their colorful pictures of the brutality of the heathen towards his women folk, this statement may seem incredible. But it is an undisputed fact of history that since the beginning of Hindu law, woman in India has held more legal rights to acquire knowledge, to hold office, and to possess property than her sisters in America are having today. She was never barred from the national institutions of higher learning because of sex, and in the development of her intellectual, moral, and spiritual qualities she was not hampered by any social or religious laws whatsoever. She has stood before law as an exact equal of man with the same rights to possess property, the same rights to go before courts of justice and to ask the protection of law. The system of coeducation prevailed in the ancient universities of Nalanda and Takhshashila. It is a familiar fact known to all western scholars that *Sakuntala*, the heroine in Kalidasa's drama of that name, pleaded her own case before the court of King Dushyanta.

[10] *Awakening of Asian Womanhood*, page 9.

Indian women have fought on battlefields alongside of men, have taken leading parts in their historic and philosophic debates, have revealed spiritual truths for the *Vedas*, and have received, as personifications of the Deity, the worship from adoring millions. Above all else, the Indian women have ruled over the hearts of their husbands and children throughout the ages with a power that is born exclusively of purity in character, and the spirit of self-sacrifice and love. They have held their dignity with a poise which does the female sex a great credit.

Does Hindu religion sanction, then, the bondage of woman, and is wife-beating permitted in Indian society? Is the Hindu wife considered merely as an instrument of pleasure, and is her whole ambition in life to be a passive and obedient servant of the husband?

The maxims which guide the conduct of Hindu society were laid down by the great Law-giver Manu, in the year 200 B. C. He says:

> "Where female relations live in grief, the family soon perishes; but that family where they are not unhappy ever prospers."
>
> "A woman's body must not be struck hard, even with a flower, because it is sacred."

That a nation which regularly listens to readings from epic poems of Ramayana and Mahabharata morning and night on every day of the year, and on whose lips the praises of Sita, the ideal wife (heroine in Ramayana), dance forever, should be carried away by the desire of ill-treating its womankind, as is actually believed by most westerners, is simply inconceivable. Sita's equal as a model of womanly chastity, uprightness, kindness, and devotion has not been known in the history of mankind. The story of her exile with her husband, King Rama, her fidelity, and her spirituality is known to every child born in India; while her character is set as an example before all Hindu women in the country. With such ideals as these constantly before their minds, and the moral influence of the peaceful, chaste family life always around them, women of any nation will develop within themselves a power which it will be impossible for any group of men, however foul and vicious, to resist. And it must be remembered that the men of India, slow as they are in catching the militaristic spirit of the competitive western life, are to an exceptional degree spiritual and religious in their general behavior. Sir Monier-Williams says:

> "Religion of some kind enters largely into their [East Indian] everyday life. Nay, it may even be said that religious ideas and aspirations—religious hopes and fears—are interwoven with the whole texture of their mental constitution. A clergyman, who has resided nearly all his life in India, once remarked to me that he had seen many a poor Indian villager whose childlike trust in his god, and in the efficacy of his religious observances—whose simplicity of character and practical application of his creed, put us Christians to shame."[11]

And again, in describing the general character of the Hindu women and their family life, he writes:

[11] Sir Monier-Williams—*Modern India and the Indians,* page 54.

"Hindu women must be allowed full credit for their strict discharge of household duties, for their personal cleanliness, thrift, activity, and practical fidelity to the doctrines and precepts of their religion. They are generally loved by their husbands, and are never brutally treated. A wife-beater drunkard is unknown in India. In return, Indian wives and mothers are devoted to their families. I have often seen wives in the act of circumambulating the sacred *Tulsi* plant 108 times, with the sole object of bringing down a blessing on their husband and children. In no other country in the world are family affection and reverence for parents so conspicuously operative as in India. In many households the first morning duty of a child on rising from sleep is to lay his head on his mother's feet in token of filial obedience. Nor could there be a greater mistake than to suppose that Indian women are without influence."[12]

[12] Sir Monier-Williams—*Modern India and the Indians,* page 318.

CHAPTER II

THE HINDU IDEAL OF MARRIAGE

Irresponsible writers have discussed the marriage system of India in so irrational and inaccurate a manner that the name *India* has become, in the mind of the westerner, synonymous with child marriage. These writers have tried to show that child marriage is the result of a law of the Hindu religion, which, according to them, strictly enjoins the parents to enforce the marriage of their daughters at a tender age under penalty of heavenly vengeance. They say that the law enjoins that girls shall be married before the age of puberty, and, as a result, the majority of Hindu girls become mothers nine months after reaching puberty. One such writer[13] picks a few lines from the Hindu poet Tagore's essay in Keyserling's *Book of Marriage,* and, mutilating its text by clever omissions, misquotes it to prove the poet a defender of child marriage. This unholy attempt of the author to misrepresent the noted poet and philosopher deserves strong censure. In this chapter we shall discuss the facts about marriage in India and its allied subject of child marriage.

The Hindu religion strictly forbids child marriage. The following quotation from the Rig Veda explains the ideal of marriage:

> "Woman is to be man's comrade in life, his *Sakhi,* with the same range of knowledge and interests, mature in body, mind and understanding, able to enter into a purposeful union on equal terms with a man of equal status, as life partner, of her own free choice, both dedicating their lifework as service to the divine Lord of the Universe, both ready to fulfil the purpose of married life from the day of marriage onward."[14]

The western method of marriage through courtship is, however, not the rule in India. Though the courtship method is being widely copied among the educated classes in the country, the prevailing custom of marriage is still through the choice of parents. In earlier times marriage by the *Svayambara* system, in which the maiden freely selected her future mate from a group of suitors, was commonly practised. This practice was discontinued, however, with the invasion of India by the foreigners because of the desire of the Indians to keep the pure Aryan stock uncontaminated by foreign blood. Since that time the boys and girls are mated through the choice of their parents. This custom may be defended on wide social and eugenic grounds. The contention is that the complete dominance of sentiment

[13] Katherine Mayo.

[14] Quoted from Cousins—*Awakening of Asian Womanhood,* page 40.

and individual desire in the courtship method of marriage, is harmful to social discipline, and is, as a rule, detrimental to the race. Marriage is a sacred bond and must be based on an ideal of the spiritual union of the souls, and not on the lower desires for sense pleasures.

In order to enable the reader to understand fully the principles underlying Hindu marriage it will be necessary to acquaint him with the fundamental characteristics which form the basis of the social structure of group life in India. One distinctive feature in the study of India is the collective character of its communal life. Hindu society was established on a basis of group morality. Society was divided into different classes or communities; "and while no absolute ethical code was held binding on all classes alike, yet within a given class (or caste) the freedom of the individual must be subordinated to the interest of the group. The concept of duty was paramount."[15] Social purpose must be served first, and the social order was placed before the happiness of the individual, whether man or woman.

In India the origin of marriage did not lie in passion. Marriage was entered into, not to satisfy desire on the part of either man or woman, but to fulfill a purpose in life. It was the duty of every individual during life to marry and propagate for the continuation of the race. His marital union did not depend upon the caprice of his will; it was required of him as a social obligation. No individual's life was considered complete without an offspring. To both man and woman marriage was the most conclusive of all incidents in life; it was the fulfillment of one's whole being. Marriage was not sought as the satisfaction of human feelings but as "the fulfilment of a ritual duty to the family in its relation to the Divine Spirit." "The happiness and fruition of family life were sought not in the tumults of passion, but in the calm and ordered affection of a disciplined and worshipful pair." That strong sexual passion which has been so beautifully sanctified by the grace of poetry and hallowed by the name of romantic love, and which is the source of immense force and power in many a young life in the West, is called by the Hindu idealist "an earthly desire and an illusion."

Love as an expression of sentiment is transitory. People who once fall in love may after some time and for similar reasons fall out of love. Hence if the ideal basis for the union of the sexes is to be mutual passion, an arrangement must be provided so that simultaneously with a break in the fascination on either side, the marriage between the parties shall come to an end. Yet under the existing conditions over the entire civilized world it would not be possible to make the marriage laws as lax as that. So long as such an arrangement remains untried, and so long as there is any truth in the statement that human hearts are to a high degree fickle, it must follow that successful marriages should have other sources of lasting satisfaction than romantic love. On observation, we find that most marriages, which were entered into on the strict principle of mutual love, hold together from habit, from considerations of prudence, and from duty towards children long after lovers' joy has totally disappeared from the lives of the couple. The glimmer of first love very soon fades into nothingness. Closer acquaintance brings to light faults which the lover's eyes in days of romance had stubbornly refused to see. Unless

[15] Coomaraswamy.

the parties are possessed of sensitive souls, unless after a serious search for a foothold they find a basis of common interest and common hobbies, and unless their mutuality of temperament is found adequate for friendship, there is left for their future relationships no happiness. Why, then, excite one's imagination in the beginning, and permit oneself to be deluded by such obviously foolish hopes?

The Hindu system of marriage reverses these considerations. There, marriage is a form of vocation, a fulfillment of a social duty, it is not the enjoyment of individual rights. In its ethics, designed for the communal basis of life, individual desire and pleasures must be subordinated to the interest of group morality. "Thus the social order is placed before the happiness of the individual, whether man or woman. This is the explanation of the greater peace which distinguishes the arranged marriage of the East from the self-chosen marriage of the West; where there is no deception there can be no disappointment."[16]

In this manner the champions of the system justify the Indian method of marriage, in which marriages are arranged by the parents or relatives. But, however ably its partisans may defend the old system, and in whatever glowing colors they may exhibit its spiritual values, it must go sooner or later. With changing times the ideals that govern Indian society have changed also. Men and women of the present day are demanding their individual freedom after the fashion of their brothers and sisters in the West. Rightly or wrongly, they feel a desire to express themselves according to the spontaneous dictates of the heart. Simultaneously with the industrialization of the country the restraints put upon the individual from outside through the medium of social and religious laws are fast disappearing. The younger generation of the Indian nation appears more concerned for rights than for duties.

Those who care may lament over the past, but we shall welcome the change with joy, because it brings new light and new hope into the stereotyped and set system of Indian life. Marriage in human society is after all nothing but a plunge into the unknown ocean of the future. Its ultimate outcome alone can tell whether the entrants were destined to sink or swim.[17] Marriage has been a lottery in the past, and it will remain so in the future, unless our lives are so modulated as to give to the forces of the spirit a larger and a freer scope. It is impious blasphemy to seek to stifle the celestial senses, instead of guiding and harmonizing them. It is hoped, however, that in their new role as imitators of the West, men of India will not change their attitude of tenderness, confidence, respect, and delicacy towards the female sex; and that the women of India will retain the calmness and dignity of their attitude, the self-respect and poise of their inner life.

All classes in India idolize motherhood. Among no people in the world are mothers more loved, honored, and obeyed than among Indians. It might be interesting to point out that a pregnant woman in India has nothing of which to be ashamed or which she wishes to hide. She is considered auspicious and must be accorded high respect and consideration. We sometimes believe that the East Indian's high good humor and calm in life are the fruits of the Indian mother's

[16] Coomaraswamy—*Dance of Siva,* page 88.
[17] Tagore.

unusual cheer and hope during the period of pregnancy. How unlike the attitude of the Indian is to the westerner's silly notions of beauty, fine shape, and grace wherein pregnancy is made an object of more or less open ridicule. Would that the women of America and other western countries would forsake their restlessness and nervousness and learn from their humbler eastern sisters the art of possessing poise, composure, and serenity! Would that they would imitate the eastern mother's delicate benevolence, generosity of heart, loftiness of mind, and independence and pride of character!

This subject of marriage is so important a matter to India that we desire to elucidate still further the ideals underlying it. We shall quote at length from Keyserling's *Book of Marriage* an essay by Tagore, than whom no one is better fitted to speak. Says Tagore:

> "Another way for the better understanding by the European of the mentality underlying our marriage system would be by reference to the discussions on eugenics which are a feature of modern Europe. The science of eugenics, like all other sciences, attaches but little weight to personal sentiment. According to it, selection by personal inclination must be rigorously regulated for the sake of the progeny. If the principle involved be once admitted, marriage needs must be rescued from the control of the heart, and brought under the province of the intellect; otherwise insoluble problems will keep on arising, for passion recks not of consequences, nor brooks interference by outside judges.
>
> "Here the question arises: If desire be banished from the very threshold of marriage, how can love find any place in the wedded life? Those who have no true acquaintance with our country, and whose marriage system is entirely different, take it for granted that the Hindu marriage is loveless. But do we not know of our own knowledge how false is such a conclusion?
>
> " ... Therefore, from their earliest years, the husband as an idea is held up before our girls, in verse and poetry, through ceremonial and worship. When at length they get this husband, he is to them not a person but a principle, like loyalty, patriotism, or such other abstractions which owe their immense strength to the fact that the best part of them is our own creation and therefore part of our own being."

The poet then offers his own personal contribution to the discussion of the marriage question generally and concludes thus:

> "This *shakti*, this joy-giving power of woman as the beloved, has up to now largely been dissipated by the greed of man, who has sought to use it for the purposes of his individual enjoyment, corrupting it, confining it, like his property, within jealously guarded limit. That has also obstructed for woman herself her inward realization of the full glory of her own *shakti*. Her person-

ality has been insulted at every turn by being made to display its power of delectation within a circumscribed arena. It is because she has not found her true place in the great world that she sometimes tries to capture man's special estate as a desperate means of coming into her own. But it is not by coming out of her home that woman can gain her liberty. Her liberation can only be effected in a society where her true *shakti*, her *ananda* (joy) is given the widest and highest scope for its activity. Man has already achieved the means of self-expansion in public activity without giving up his individual concerns. When, likewise, any society shall be able to offer a larger field for the creative work of woman's special faculty, without detracting from her creative work in the home, then in such society will the true union of man and woman become possible.

"The marriage system all over the world, from the earliest ages till now, is a barrier in the way of such true union. That is why woman's *shakti*, in all existing societies, is so shamefully wasted and corrupted. That is why in every country marriage is still more or less of a prison-house for the confinement of women—with all its guards wearing the badge of the dominant male. That is why man, by dint of his efforts to bind woman, has made her the strongest of fetters for his own bondage. That is why woman is debarred from adding to the spiritual wealth of society by the perfection of her own nature, and all human societies are weighed down with the burden of the resulting poverty.

"The civilization of man has not, up to now, loyally recognized the reign of the spirit. Therefore the married state is still one of the most fruitful sources of the unhappiness and downfall of woman, of his disgrace and humiliation. But those who believe that society is a manifestation of the spirit will assuredly not rest in their endeavors till they have rescued human marriage relations from outrage by the brute forces of society—till they have thereby given free play to the force of love in all the concerns of humanity."

Such is the Hindu poet's explanation of the ideals underlying the institution of marriage in the communal society of the Hindus. One feels through his closing lines the poet's sorrow at the sight of the misery caused by a wrong conception of marriage throughout the civilized world. The poet cherishes, however, the fond hope that a day of the reign of spirit will dawn over the world, when mankind will recognize the necessity of giving to the forces of love a free play in the wide concerns of life.

Marriage in India involves two separate ceremonies. The first ceremony is the more elaborate, and judging from the permanent character of its obligations, the more important. It is performed amid much festivity and show. The bridal party, consisting of the bridegroom with his chief relatives and friends, goes to the bride's home in an elaborate musical procession. There the party is handsomely feasted as guests of the bride for one or more days, according to the means of the host. The groom furnishes the entertainment, which consists of music, acrobatic dancing, jugglers' tricks, fireworks, and so forth. The day is spent in simple outdoor amusements like hunting, horseback riding, swimming, or gymnastic plays, the nature of the sport depending upon the surroundings. In the evening, by the light of the fireworks, and in the midst of a large crowd of near relatives and spectators, the ceremony of the "union," namely, the spiritual unification of the near relatives of the bride and the bridegroom, is staged in a highly picturesque manner. In order of their relation to the bride and groom—father of the bride with the father of the bridegroom, first uncle of the one with the first uncle of the other, and so forth—the near relatives of the future couple embrace each other and exchange head-dresses as a symbol of eternal friendship. Each such pledge of friendship is beautifully harmonized with a song and a blessing from the daughters of the village. Later in the evening, the girls lead the guests to the bridal feast, singing in chorus on their march the "Welcome Home."

Marriage in the Indian home is thus an occasion of great rejoicing. The atmosphere that prevails throughout the entire ceremony is one of extreme wholesomeness and joy. Nothing could surpass the loveliness and charm that surrounds the evening march to the bridal feast. The pretty maidens of the village, who are conscious of their dignity as personifications of the Deity and are inspired with a devoted love for their sister bride, come in their gay festival dresses, with mingled feelings of pride and modesty, to lead the procession with a song; their eyes moistened with slowly gathering tears of deep and chaste emotion, and their faces wrapped in ever changing blushes, give to the whole picture a distinctive flavor of an inspiring nature. On the following morning the couple are united in marriage by the officiating priest, who reads from the scriptures while the husband and wife pace together the seven steps. The vow of equal comradeship which is taken by both the husband and the wife on this occasion reads thus:

> "Become thou my partner, as thou hast paced all the seven steps with me.... Apart from thee I cannot live. Apart from me do thou not live. We shall live together; we each shall be an object of love to the other; we shall be a source of joy each unto the other; with mutual goodwill shall we live together."[18]

The marriage ceremony being over, the bridal party departs with the bride for the bridegroom's home. On this first trip the bride is accompanied by a maid, and the two return home together after an overnight's stay. The bride then remains at her parental home until the performance of the second ceremony. The interval between the two ceremonies varies from a few days to several years, depending mainly upon the ages of the married couple and the husband's ability to support a home.

This dual ceremonial has been the cause of a great deal of confusion in the western mind. To all appearances the first ceremony is the more important as it is termed marriage. After it the bride begins to dress and behave like a married

[18] Quoted from Cousins—*The Awakening of Asian Womanhood,* page 38.

woman, but the couple do not begin to live together until the second ceremony has also been performed, and these two acts may be separated from each other by a considerably long period. In other words the so-called marriage of the Hindu girl is nothing but "an indefeasible betrothal in the western sense." The custom of early marriage (or betrothal, to be more exact) has existed in some parts of the country from earlier times, but it became more common during the period of the Mohammedan invasions into India. These foreign invaders were in the habit of forcibly converting to Islam the beautiful Hindu maidens, whom they later married. But no devout Mohammedan ever injures or thinks evil towards a married woman. His religion strictly forbids such practice. Thus, to safeguard the honor of their young daughters the Hindus adopted this custom of early marriage.

The girl's marriage, however, makes no change in her life. She continues to live with her parents as before, and is there taught under her mother's supervision the elementary duties of a household. She is instructed at the same time in other matters concerning a woman's life. When she becomes of an age to take upon herself the responsibilities of married life, the second marriage ceremony is finished and she departs for her new home.

It is true that the standard of education among East Indian women as compared with that of other countries is appallingly low. We shall leave the discussion of the various political factors which have contributed to this deplorable state of things for a later chapter. For the present it will be sufficient to point out that even though the Indian girl is illiterate and unable to read and write, she is not uninstructed or uninformed in the proper sense of the word education.

She knows how to cook, to sew, to embroider, and to do every other kind of household work. She is fully informed concerning matters of hygiene and sex. In matters intellectual her mind is developed to the extent that "she understands thoroughly the various tenets of her religion and is quite familiar with Hindu legends and the subject matter in the epic literature of India."

My mother was the daughter of a village carpenter. She was brought up in the village under the exclusive guidance of her mother and did not have any school education. Mother, in her turn, has reared seven children who have all grown to be perfectly healthy and normal boys and girls. Even though we could easily afford a family doctor, we never had one. Mother seemed to know so much about hygienic and medical science that she did not need a doctor. Her little knowledge she had acquired from her own mother; it consisted of a few simple rules, which she observed very faithfully. As little children, we were required to clean our teeth with a fresh twig, to be individually chewed into a brush, every morning before breakfast, and to wash the mouth thoroughly with water after each meal. For the morning teeth cleaning we were supplied with twigs from a special kind of tree which leaves in the mouth a very pleasant taste and contains juices of a beneficial nature. Also, chewing a small twig every morning gives good exercise to the teeth and furnishes the advantage of a new brush each time. We were told that dirty teeth were unmannerly and hurt a person's eyesight and general heath. A cold water bath once a day and washing of both hands before and after each meal were other fundamental requirements.

For every kind of family sickness, whether it was a headache, a fever, a cold in the head, or a bad cough, the prescription was always the same. A mixture of simple herbs was boiled in water and given to the patient for drinking. Its only effect was a motion of the bowels. It was not a purgative, but had very mild and wholesome laxative properties without any after reactions. Fasting during sickness was highly recommended. In nearly every month occurred some special festival day on which the whole family fasted. This fast had a purifying effect on the systems of growing children. As another precautionary measure, my mother prepared for the children, every winter, a special kind of preserve from a bitter variety of black beans, which is supposed to possess powerful blood-purifying properties. With the exception of quinine during malarial epidemics, we were never given any drugs whatsoever. These simple medicines, combined with a fresh vegetable diet for every day in the year, constituted my mother's only safeguards against family sickness. And from my knowledge I know that her system worked miraculously well.

During pregnancy it is customary to surround the young girl with every precaution. She returns to her parental home in order to secure freedom from sexual intercourse during that period. In the months before my eldest sister bore her first child, I remember how she was instructed not to permit herself to be excited in any way. Pictures of the ideal wife, *Sita*, and of national heroes and heroines were hung all over the house for my sister to look at and admire. She was freed from all household responsibilities in order that she could devote her time to reading good stories from the Hindu epics. Every kind of irritant, like pepper and spices, was rigidly excluded from her diet, and after the child was born she refrained from injudicious combinations of food until the child was a year or more old.

Every night at bedtime my mother had a new story to tell the children, a story which she herself had heard at bedtime when she was young. These stories were drawn from the great Hindu epics, and there was always a useful maxim connected with them. The tale was told to bring home to the growing children some moral maxim like truthfulness, fidelity to a pledge once given, conjugal happiness, and respect for parents. In this manner the children in the most ignorant homes become familiar with the ethical teachings of their nation and with the hypotheses underlying their respective religions. Almost everyone in India down to the most ignorant countrywoman understands the subtle meaning of such intricate Hindu doctrines as the laws of *Karma*, the theory of reincarnation, and the philosophy of *Maya*.

As was stated earlier in this chapter, much misinformation about the so-called child marriage has been spread by ignorant missionaries, and has been eagerly swallowed by most western readers. It may be well to observe here that the two expressions "child marriage" and "early marriage" are very widely apart in meaning. The psychological impressions conveyed by the two expressions are distinctly different. If the first ceremony of the Hindu marriage is to be taken as meaning marriage, what is practised in India perhaps more than anywhere else in the world is *early marriage* and not child marriage. Even at that, early marriage is essentially wrong in principle. Its usefulness in earlier times, when it was first recommended by the Hindu lawgivers as a necessary measure to preserve the communal life of the nation, cannot be denied.

Like many other laws of those times, it has outlived its usefulness, and through the influence of many corruptions which have been added to the practice during ages, it has become a curse to the country. This fact is frankly admitted by the leaders of modern India. In the writings and speeches of the most prominent among them the custom of early marriage has been condemned as a "deadly vermin in Hindu social life," and a "ghastly form of injustice." Beginning with the days of the eminent Hindu reformer Raja Ram Mohan Roy, the whole literature of social and religious reform in India is full of loud and emphatic denunciations of early marriage.

As a result of the untiring, self-sacrificing efforts of Hindu reformers a great measure of success has already been achieved. The Hindu girl's age of marriage has been steadily increasing during the last fifty years. According to figures from the official Census Report of India (1921) only 399 out of every 1000 girls were married at the end of their fifteenth year. In other words, 60 per cent of Indian girls remained unmarried at the beginning of their sixteenth year. Moreover, in the official records of India every girl who has passed through the first ceremony of her marriage is included in the married class. If we allow a little further concession on account of the warmer climate of India, which has the tendency to lower the age of maturity in girls, we shall concede that the present conditions in India in respect to early marriage are not strikingly different from those in most European countries. At the same time it must not be forgotten that in India sex life begins invariably after marriage, and never before marriage. Those familiar with the conditions in the western countries know that such is not always the rule there.

One evening the writer was talking in rather favorable terms to a small group of friends about the Hindu system of marriage. While several nodded their habitual, matter-of-fact, courteous assent, one young lady (Dorothy), a classmate and an intimate friend, suddenly said in an impatient tone, "This is all very foolish. By using those sweet expressions in connection with the Hindu family life you do not mean to tell me that marriage between two strangers, who have never met in life before, or known each other, can be ever happy or just. 'Felicity,' 'peace,' 'harmony,' 'wedded love,' 'idealization of the husband'—this is all bunk. That *you* should approve the blindfold yoking together for life of innocent children in indefeasible marriage, is outrageous. The system is shocking; it is a sin against decency. It is war against the most sacred of human instincts and emotions, and as such I shall condemn it as criminal and uncivilized." Yet the young lady was in no sense of the word unsympathetic or unfriendly to India. She is, and has always been, a great friend and admirer of India.

Dorothy is not much of a thinker, but she is very liberal and likes to be called a radical. You could discuss with her any subject whatsoever, even Free Love and Birth Control, with perfect ease and lack of restraint. She is twenty-five years of age and unmarried. She has been "in love" several times, but for one reason or the other she has not yet found her ideal man. She would not tell this to everybody, but to one of her boy friends, "whose big blue eyes had poetic inspiration in them," and who seemed to be fine and good and true in every way, better than the best she had ever met before, and whom she loved quite genuinely, she had given herself completely on one occasion. This happened during a week-end trip to the mountains, and was the first and last of her sexual experience. She said it was the moral as well as the physical feast of her life. Later she saw him flirting in a doubtful manner with a coarse Spanish girl, which made him loathsome in her eyes. Gradually her love for him began to dwindle, until it died off completely, leaving behind, however, a deep mortal scar in her spiritual nature. For a period, Dorothy thought she could never love any man again, until she began to admire a young college instructor in a mild fashion. He is, however, "so kind and intelligent and different from the rest," with a fine physique and handsome face—his powerful forehead setting so beautifully against his thick curly hair—that she calls magnificent. It matters little that he is married, because she writes him the most enchanting letters. Dorothy's love for the handsome professor is platonic. She says it will exist forever, even though she entertains no hope of ever marrying him. Yet while she talked about her latest "ideal," a stream of tears gathered slowly in her big luminous eyes. They were the tears of hopeless resignation. Dorothy is beautiful, and possesses rare grace and charm of both body and mind. She is well situated in the business world, and is not in want of men admirers. But yet she is unhappy, extremely unhappy. She has had the freedom, but no training to make proper use of it. While she was still in her early teens she started going on picnic parties with different boys. Under the impulse of youthful passion she learned to kiss any one and every one in an indiscriminate fashion. This destroyed the sanctity of her own moral and spiritual nature, and also killed, at the same time, her respect for the male sex. Sacredness of sex and respect for man being thus destroyed in her early years, she could not easily find an ideal husband in later life. If she had been a stupid creature with no imagination and no deep finer feelings she would have fallen suddenly in love anywhere—there to pass the rest of her humdrum and joyless existence in an everlasting stupor. Surely Dorothy did not remember her own tragedy when she condemned the lot of the Hindu girls in such vehement manner. Vanity is an ugly fault, yet it gives great pleasure.

Unlike India, where from their very childhood girls are initiated into matters of sex, and where the ideal of acquiring a husband and a family is kept before their minds from the beginning, American boys and girls are brought up in utter ignorance of every thing pertaining to sex. Sex is considered as something unclean, filthy, and nauseous, and so unworthy of the attention and thought of young children. And yet there is no country in the world where sex is kept more prominently before the public eye in every walk of daily life than in America. *The first impression which a stranger landing in America gets is of the predominance of sex in its daily life.* The desire of the American woman to show her figure to what Americans call "the coarse eye of man," expresses itself in short skirts and tight dresses. "American movies are made with no other purpose in view than to emphasize sex." A college professor was recently told by one of the six biggest directors of motion pictures in Hollywood, through whose hands passed a business amounting to millions of dollars, that in making a motion picture sex must constantly be borne in mind. The story must be based on that knowledge, scenes selected with this view, and the plot executed with that thought in mind. Vaudeville shows, one of America's national amusements, are nothing but a suggestive display of the beautiful legs of young girls, who appear on the stage scantily dressed and touch their foreheads with the toes in a highly suggestive manner.

The writer was told by an elderly American lady that the American national dances had a deep religious connotation. A spiritual thought may exist behind American music, and its effect on the American youth may be quite uplifting, but certainly such dances as the one called "Button shining dance," in which a specially close posture is necessary, was invented with no high spiritual end in view. A wholesale public display of bare legs to the hips, and a close view of the rest of their bodies in tight bathing suits may be seen on the national beaches. Young couples lie on the sands in public view closely locked in seemingly everlasting embraces.

While all this may be very pure, innocent, harmless, and even uplifting in its hidden nature, its outward and more prevalent character indicates an almost vicious result of the ideal of bringing up the nation's youth improperly instructed in matters of sex and its proper function.

The immediate effect of this anomalous condition in America resulting from the misinstruction regarding sex by its youth on the one hand, and the most exaggerated prominence given sex in its national life is particularly disastrous and excessively humiliating. Using the word moral in its popular conventional meaning, it may be very frankly said that the morals of the American youth are anything but exemplary. Judge Ben B. Lindsey, who is fully authorized to speak on the subject from his experience as head of the Juvenile court in Denver for over twenty-five years, and who is one of the keenest contemporary thinkers in America, has stated facts in his book, *The Revolt of Modern Youth,* which are appalling. He writes:

> "The first item in the testimony of the high school students is that of all the youth who go to parties, attend dances, and ride together in automobiles, more than 90 per cent indulge in hugging and kissing. This does not mean that every girl lets *any* boy hug and kiss her, but that she *is* hugged and kissed.
>
> "The second part of the message is this. At least 50 per cent of those who begin with hugging and kissing do not restrict themselves to that, but go further, and indulge in other sex liberties which, by all the conventions, are outrageously improper.
>
> "Now for the third part of the message. It is this: Fifteen to twenty-five per cent of those who begin with the hugging and kissing eventually 'go the limit.' This does not, in most cases, mean either promiscuity or frequency, but it happens."[19]

This situation is alarming, and the leaders of the country must take immediate notice of it. When fifteen to twenty-five girls out of every hundred in any country indulge in irresponsible sexual relationships between the ages of fifteen and eighteen, that country is not in a healthy moral condition. The effect of these early

[19] Pages 56, 59, 62.

sexual intimacies between young girls and boys is ruinous to their later spiritual growth. How the situation may be remedied is a serious problem, which is not the task of any foreigner, however honest and friendly, to solve.

It may be of value to point out here how the Hindu thinkers sought to control this situation. We quoted above the frank opinion of an American college girl regarding the Hindu system of marriage. The ill opinion of the Hindu system of marriage held by most westerners, springs, however, not from their knowledge of the situation, but from its very novelty, and from the dissociation of the name romance from its system. The western method of marriage emphasizes freedom for the individual, and as such its fundamental basis is both noble and praiseworthy. From the exercise of freedom have developed some of the finest traits of character; freedom, in fact, has been the source of inspiration for the highest achievements of the human race. But freedom in sex relationship without proper knowledge transforms itself into license, as its exercise in the commercial relationships of the world without sympathy and vision develops into tyranny. An illustration of the former consequence may be seen in the disastrous effect of the wrong kind of freedom on the morals of the American youth; the slums of the industrial world are the results of the *laissez faire* policy when it is allowed to proceed unchecked, on its reckless career.

In India marriage is regarded as a necessity in life; in the case of woman it is the most conclusive of all incidents, the one action to which all else in life is subsidiary. From marriage springs not only her whole happiness, but on it also depends the fulfilment of her very life. Marriage to a woman is a sacrament—an entrance into the higher and holier regions of love and consecration—and motherhood is to her a thing of pride and duty. From childhood she has been trained to be the ideal of the husband whom marriage gives her. Dropping longingly into the embrace of her husband with almost divine confidence in his protection and love, she begins to look at the whole universe in a different light. "Are the heavens and the earth so suddenly transformed? Do the birds and trees, the stars and the heavens above, take on a more brilliant coloring, and the wind begin to murmur a sweeter music?" Or is it true that she is herself transformed at the gentle touch of him who is henceforth to be her lord?

So limitless is the power of human emotion that we can create in our own imagination scenes of a joyful existence, which, when they are finally realized, bring about miraculous changes in us almost overnight. This miracle is no fiction; it is a reality. An overnight's blissful acquaintance with her husband has altered the constitution of many a girl's body and given to her figure nobler curves. I have seen my own sister given in marriage, a girl of 18, a slender, playful, fond child with barely a sign of womanhood in her habits and carriage; and after a month when I went for a visit to her home I found it difficult to recognize my own sister. How suddenly had the marital union transformed her! In the place of a slender, sprightly girl was now a plump woman with a blooming figure, seeming surcharged with radiant energy; in the place of a straight childish look in the eyes there was a look of happiness, wisdom, understanding that was inspiring and ennobling. The atmosphere around my sister, once a girl, now a woman, was of such a divine character and her appearance expressed such exquisite joy that I fell spontaneously into her arms, and before we separated our eyes were wet with tears of joy. Seeing my sister so beautiful and so happy, I was happy; and in her moment of supreme joy her brother, the beloved companion of early days, became doubly dear to her. Some moments in our lives are difficult, nay, impossible to forget. This experience was of so illuminating a nature that it is still as vivid in my mind as if it had happened yesterday.

The explanation is very simple. In the mind of my sister, as in the mind of every other Indian girl, the idea of a husband had been uppermost since her very childhood. Around his noble appearance, fine carriage, and handsome expression she must have woven many a beautiful story. Each time she saw one of her girl friends given in marriage to a "flower-crowned bridegroom, dressed in saffron-colored clothes, riding in procession on a decorated horse," and accompanied by music and festivity, she must have dreamed. And then when the ideal of her childhood was realized, no wonder she found in his company that height of emotional exaltation which springs from the proper union of the sexes and is the noblest gift of God to man. The American girl thinks my sister married a stranger, but she had married an ideal, a creation of her imagination, and a part of her own being.

The wise Hindu system which keeps the idea of a husband before the girls from their childhood will not be easily understood by the conventional western mind. Those who consider sex as something "unclean and filthy" and have formed the conviction that its thoughts and its very name must be strictly kept away from growing children must learn two fundamental truths. In the first place, nothing in sex is filthy or unclean; on the other hand, sex is "the purest and the loveliest thing in life and if properly managed is emotionally exalting and highly uplifting for our moral and spiritual development."[20] Secondly, to imagine that by maintaining a conspiracy of silence on the subject of sex one can exclude its thought totally from the lives of growing children is to betray in the grossest form ignorance of natural laws.

In India, however, sex is considered a necessary part of a healthy individual's life; it is a sacred and a lovely thing; and, as such, it is to be carefully examined and carefully cultivated. The sexual impulse is recognized as the strongest of human impulses, and any attempt to thwart it by outside force must result in disaster to the individual and in ruin to social welfare. To overcome sex hunger by keeping people ignorant of it is the meanest form of hypocrisy. To deny facts is not to destroy them. It is not only stupid but cowardly to imagine that one could make people moral and spiritual by keeping them ignorant and superstitious. Show them the light, and they will find their own way. Teach children the essentials of life, encourage in them the habit of independent thought, show them by example and precept the beauties of moral grandeur, and they will develop within themselves the good qualities of self-respect and self-restraint which will further insure against many pitfalls. Says the Hindu proverb: "A woman's best guard is her own virtue." Virtue is a thing which must spring from within and can never be imposed from the outside.

[20] Ben B. Lindsey.

The atmosphere in the Hindu household and the attitude of the elder members of the family to each other is of such a nature that the boys and girls gradually become aware of the central facts of nature. In fact, no attempt is made to hide from the children anything about their life functions. The subjects of marriage and child birth are freely discussed in the family gatherings. Children are never excluded when a brother or sister is born, and no one tells them stories of little babies brought in baskets by the doctors or by storks. Whenever the growing children ask curious questions about physiological facts, they are given the necessary information to the extent that it will be intelligible to them.

The experience in India has clearly demonstrated the fact that if young boys and girls are properly instructed in the laws of nature, and if the knowledge is backed up by the right kind of moral stimulus and idealism, these young people can be relied upon to develop invincible powers of self-restraint and self-respect. Such boys and girls will have noble aspirations and will grow into fine-spirited men and women of healthy moral character and of unquestionable poise.

The writer has no desire to eulogize the Hindu system of marriage, or to disparage the Occidental. An attempt has been made to diagnose the prevalent consequences of two systems. The Hindu customs certainly need modification in view of the rapid economic and social changes; the western system displays a deplorable lack of adjustment to new conditions in those countries. The writer merely asks the reader to remember that just because a system is different, it need not be outrageous.

CHAPTER III

THE CIVILIZATION AND ETHICS OF INDIA

The distinctive feature of Hindu culture is its femininity. While the northern branch of the Aryan family represented by the European group had to undergo hard struggle with unyielding nature on account of a barren soil and the severity of cold climate, which developed in them the masculine qualities of aggressiveness, force, and exertion, the southern branch of the Aryan family, who migrated into the smiling valleys of the Indus and the Ganges, found in their new home abundance of physical comfort. The extreme fertility of soil and the warm climate made existence easy and left them leisure for speculation and thought—conditions which have tended to make the people of India emotional, meditative, and mystic. The bounty of nature released them from struggle, and the resulting freedom from material cares and security of existence developed in the Hindu character the benevolent qualities of tolerance and thankfulness.[21]

The peace-loving nature of the Hindu mind shows itself in its early ventures into the study of the higher and deeper problems of life. When they began to inquire into the secrets of the universe and its relationship to human life with a view to discovering the mystery of our existence on this planet, they were dominated solely by an absolute and unqualified love of truth. "They never quarreled about their beliefs or asked any questions about individual faiths. Their only ambition was to acquire knowledge of the universe,—of its origin and cause,—and to understand the whence and whither, the who and what of the human soul." The early pioneers of Hindu thought lay down for rest on the open, fertile plains of the Ganges during the fragrant summer nights of India, and their eyes sought the starry heavens above. Then they looked into themselves, and must have asked, "What are we? What is this life on earth meant for? How did we come here? Where are we bound for? What becomes of the human soul?" and many another difficult question. The answer that the Hindu sages of old gave to these difficult questions is to be found in the one simple rule of the Unity of All Life: One Supreme Being is the source of all joy; He is the master of all knowledge; He is eternal, stainless, unchangeable, and always present as a witness in every conscience; He alone is real and lasting, and the rest of this material universe is *maya,* a mere illusion. Human soul is made of the same substance as the Supreme soul. It is separated from its source through ignorance. Through succeeding incarnations it strives to reach its ultimate goal, which is its identification with the Supreme Being. That is the final end of all human effort—the realization of the Self—which accomplished, man's

[21] Max Müller.

existence becomes one with the rest of the Universe, and his life thereafter is one of limitless love. His soul unites with the Universal soul and he has obtained his *Moksha* (*salvation*). He begins to see "All things in self and self in All."

This idea of spiritual freedom, which is the release of the self from the ego concept, forms the foundation of Hindu culture, and has influenced the whole character of India's social and religious ideals. Let us try to explain it a little more clearly. The recognition of the unity of all life assumes the existence of one God, "one source, one essence and one goal." The final purpose of life is to realize this unity, when the human soul becomes one with the Universal Spirit. Ignorance is the cause of all evil, because it forever hides from us the true vision. The wise man continually strives to overcome ignorance through the study of philosophy and through self-restraint and renunciation. He seeks to achieve knowledge of Self, in order that he may see God face to face. Then he will attain *Moksha* (salvation). Until he has realized the absolute Truth, he must hold on to the relative truth as he sees it, which is accomplished through the exercise of such virtues as universal love, faith, devotion, self-sacrifice, and renunciation.

"Despising everything else, a wise man should strive after the knowledge of the Self."

Human life on this earth is a journey from one village to the other. We are all pilgrims here, and this abode is only our temporary home and not a permanent residence. Instead of being continually in search of material wealth, of power, of fame, and of toiling day and night, why should we not regard life as a perpetual holiday and learn to rest and enjoy it? Would it not be better if we had a little less of work, a little less of so-called pleasure, and more of thought and peace? It does not take much to sustain life; vegetable food in small quantities will maintain the body in good health, and the shelter of a cottage is all that a man requires. That he should build palaces and amass riches proves his lack of knowledge; that he should try to find happiness from the ruin of the happiness of his fellow beings, the inevitable consequence of the building up of great fortunes, is absurd. Nothing is real except His law and His power. Human life, like a bubble on the surface of a mighty ocean, may burst and disappear at any moment. "There is fruit on the trees in every forest, which everyone who likes may pluck without trouble. There is cool and sweet water in the pure rivers here and there. There is a soft bed made of the twigs of the beautiful creepers. And yet wretched people suffer pain at the door of the rich."

> "A man seeking for eternal happiness (moksha) might obtain it by a hundredth part of the suffering which a foolish man endures in the pursuit of riches."
>
> "Poor men eat more excellent bread than the rich; for hunger gives it sweetness."

Thus the doctrine of Maya has taught the people of India that all material things are illusion.

Thus, guided by the vision of Universal Spirit, which sustains the entire creation, and saved by the right comprehension of the doctrine of Maya, the Hindus have developed a civilization in which people are inspired largely by the ideals of human fellowship, by love and by spiritual comfort. The wisdom of the Hindu's retiring, passive attitude toward life will not readily be acknowledged by his sturdy, aggressive, and combative brothers in the western world. The Occidental's necessities of life have assumed such immense proportions, and social relations have become so intricate and insecure, that a man's whole life is spent in making sure of mere existence, and in providing against the accidents of the future. Such is the deadening influence of the continual hurly-burly of every-day life around him, that he has begun to regard life as synonymous with work. He has never himself tasted the sweetness of security and peace, and when he hears anyone else discuss it, he is likely to brand the doctrine as dreamy, unreal, and impractical. "But is it surely wise to destroy the best objects of life for the sake of life? Is the winning of wealth and the enjoying of pleasure always a superior choice to that of spiritual freedom?" To love leisure, ideals, and peace has been the criterion of Hindu wisdom. Those who have closely studied the history of the Hindu nation know the illumination, the peace, the joy, the strength that its lessons bring into the lives of those simple, virtuous people.

Hindu civilization has been, on the whole, humane and wholesome, and the life of the people of India has been one of unalloyed usefulness and service to humanity. India has always been the home of various religions and its people have always been divided into innumerable faiths. At no period of its long history, however, has religious persecution been practised by any class of people in the country. "No war was ever waged in or outside of India by the Hindu nation in the name of religion. India has never witnessed the horrors of an inquisition; no holy wars were undertaken, and no heretics burned alive for the protection of religion." In the entire history of the Hindu nation, not a drop of blood has ever been shed in the name of religion. To those who have read the accounts of the bloody tortures and the massacres that have been enacted for the sake of religion among the Christian nations of the world, this *is saying much.*

The hobby of the Hindu is not Catholicism, Presbyterianism, Methodism, or any other form of ism known to the western world; his interest does not lie in Hinduism, Buddhism, or Sikhism. His passion is for religion. "He loves not *a* religion; *he lives for religion.*" It was his love of religion which an old English missionary found among the inhabitants of a small village in Northern India. Tired from walking in the hot summer sun, this wandering friar lay down under the cool shade of a banyan tree for rest, and fell asleep. How long he slept and what brilliant dreams of His Master Lord Christ's mercy this humble mendicant had, no one knows. When in the late afternoon he opened his eyes, he saw a beautiful young girl gently fanning his face, while her little brother stood near, carrying in his arms a basket of choice fruits and a jug of fresh, cool water. As the old friar's eyes finally met the maiden's kindly gaze, he exclaimed: "At last after all these weary travels I have found a Christian people!"

Religion to the Hindu is not one among the many interests in life. It is the all-absorbing interest. The thought of a Universal Brotherhood taught in his religion guides every social, commercial, and political act of his life; while the hope of divine sanction inspires his efforts in the intellectual and spiritual spheres. Religion is not the mere profession of a certain theological faith, whose ritual may be observed on appointed occasions and then be forgotten till time again comes for worship and prayer. Religion is the "Yearning beyond" on the part of man, and when once its essence is realized, the spirit must influence every interest of the individual's life. This is the way in which religion is understood in India. "It is not a matter of form, but of mind and will. To the Hindu, it is more religious to cleanse the soul and build a good character than to mutter prayers and observe a strict ritual. Morality should form the basis of religion, and emphasis should be laid, not on outward observance, but on inward spiritual culture."

> "By deed, thought, and word, one should do good to (all) living beings. This Harsha declared to be the highest way of earning religious merit."

The main purpose of life is the realization of Self, to which all other interests must be completely subordinated. The material things of the world are but a means to this end; and the end being religion, its thought must not be lost sight of in arranging the details of life. Hence, religion pervades the entire fabric of Hindu society. Study Indian art, law, ethics, and political economy; everywhere you will find the same thought of God and his all-embracing mercy underlying them all.

The religion of the holy Jesus, who taught the doctrine of non-resistance and whose Sermon on the Mount is resplendent with love for humanity, has inspired many a Gandhi in the East. It has, however, been the cause of much bloodshed and slaughter. Under its banner slavery was sustained until the economic conditions throughout the world made its abolition inevitable and imperative. The negro-traffic, involving human brutality which makes us shudder and horrors which freeze our blood and leave us aghast, was carried on by Christian people with the express sanction of the most holy See and her august lieutenants of God. As late as the end of the nineteenth century China was subdued in the name of Christian religion. The immediate provocation of the Boxer War was the murder of two white missionaries in the interior of China. What deeds of chivalry the soldiers of the western nations, who were sent to China for the defence of Christianity, did, are recorded by Mr. Gowen in his *An Outline History of China* thus:

> "But in Tung Chow alone, a city where the Chinese made no resistance and where there was no fighting, five hundred and seventy-three women of the upper classes committed suicide rather than survive the indignities they had suffered. Our civilization of which we boast so much is still something of a veneer."

The religion of the Hindu requires him to practise love toward his fellow-man, tenderness toward animal life, and toleration of religious diversities with other people. He believes that the Christians, the Mohammedans, and the Jews may be as good men in their human relationships as he and be on as straight a road to heaven as he is. He does not question the divine revelation of the holy books of other religions, nor does he deny "that Christ was the Son of God, and Mohammed the Prophet of God." All that he wishes in this life is that he should be allowed to worship his Deity as he chooses. Says Krishna in Bhagvat Gita, the Bible of the Hindus: "Whosoever come to Me, through whatever form, through that I reach him; All men are struggling to reach Me through various paths, and all the paths are Mine."

"There is in the Hindu religion a doctrine called *Ahimsa,* namely, non-injury to any form of life, which transcends any ethical ideal known to the western ethics. The idea finds expression in the Society for Prevention of Cruelty to Children and Animals." The Hindu religion is the only religion in the world which forbids the eating of animal flesh. If all life is of one essence, if the animal pleading for life suffers as truly as man under the same conditions, is it fair to kill the animal for the sake of a simple pleasure? This gentle doctrine of harmlessness has helped to develop in the Hindu character the noble virtues of benevolence and universal love. The Hindu may lack the so-called "manly virtues"; his spiritual nature may be shocked to hear that perfectly civilized men and women kill animals for sport, that they go on pleasure excursions on the ocean to shoot the flying fish. The fish is harmless, and when shot merely falls into the ocean; merely in shooting it lies the sportsman's amusement. Which of the two extreme doctrines is right, we shall leave the reader to judge for himself. But the general doctrine of "harmlessness" must commend itself to the enlightened moral sense of the West. A right comprehension of this principle will assist greatly in getting rid of the curse of cruelty and war.

Two features in the Hindu character which stand out most conspicuously are truthfulness and chivalry towards women. The name for truth in the Sanscrit language is *satya,* which means *to be.* "So truth in the Hindu's language means that which is. It may not necessarily be the same as that which is believed by the majority of people. Again, the highest praise given to the gods in the Veda is that they are truthful and trustworthy. We know that people will ascribe to their gods the same qualities which are held in highest regard among themselves. The whole literature of ancient and modern India is full of episodes proclaiming the virtue of truth. Rama's answer to Bharata in the epic poem of *Ramayna* [quoted on page 3] is typical of the Hindu's regard for truth. In Mahabharata again we find the same devotion to a pledge once given. Bhisma, for example, was willing to suffer death rather than to disregard his pledge never to hurt a woman. The poets of the Vedas, the sages of Upnishads, and the writers of the law books were all inspired by feelings of profound love and reverence for truth. The whole literature of India is vibrant with the same keynote—highest regard for truth."[22] A perusal of the accounts of the character and culture of the people of India left by foreign travelers in ancient and modern times shows that the traveler was most deeply impressed in each instance by the Hindu's love of truth. Let us examine a few of these accounts.

The Chinese traveler Hiouen-thsang writes:

> "Though the Indians are of a light temperament, they are distinguished by the straightforwardness and honesty of their character. With regard to riches, they never take anything unjustly; with regard to justice, they make even excessive concessions....

[22] Max Müller.

Straightforwardness is the distinguishing feature of their administration."[23]

The Mohammedan historian, Idris, writes thus in his Geography (11th century):

> "The Indians are naturally inclined to justice, and never depart from it in their actions. Their good faith, honesty, and fidelity to their engagements are well known, and they are so famous for these qualities that people flock to their country from every side."[24]

Marco Polo, the Venetian explorer, says:

> "You must know that these Abraiaman (Brahman) are the best merchants in the world, and the most truthful, for they would not tell a lie for anything on earth."[25]

Major-General Sir W. H. Sleeman, K. C. B., who resided in India nearly a quarter of a century, and who was during this period employed in various capacities in which he came in direct contact with hundreds of people every day, writes of the Indians thus:

> "I have had before me hundreds of cases in which a man's property, liberty, or life depended upon his telling a lie, and he has refused to tell it."

At another place while speaking about the Indian merchants Major Sleeman says:

> "I believe there is no class of men in the world more strictly honorable in their dealings than the mercantile classes of India. Under native government a merchant's books were appealed to as 'holy writ,' and the confidence in them has certainly not diminished under our rule."

Finally we shall quote from a speech made by Sir Guy Fleetwood Wilson in 1913 when he was retiring from the high office of Finance Member of the Indian Government:

> "I wish to pay a tribute to the Indians whom I know best. The Indian officials, high and low, of my department, through the years of my connection with them, have proved themselves to be unsparing of service and absolutely trustworthy. As for their trustworthiness, let me give an instance. Three years ago, when it fell to my lot to impose new taxes, it was imperative that their nature should remain secret until they were officially announced. Everybody in the department had to be entrusted with this secret. Any one of these, from high officials to low-paid compositors of the Government Press, would have become a millionaire by using

[23] Quoted from Max Müller.
[24] Quoted from Max Müller.
[25] Quoted from Max Müller.

> the secret improperly. But even under such tremendous temptation no one betrayed his trust."[26]

Comment after these unequivocal testimonies of eminent foreign chroniclers of India is unnecessary. Where else in the world could the experience of the Finance Member Sir Guy Wilson be repeated? If everyone who visited the country was equally impressed by the truthful character of the Hindus there must surely be meaning in the statement that the Hindus are honest, truthful, and straightforward. Foreign travelers have visited other lands during various historical periods, but nowhere else were they so singularly impressed by the integrity of the people as in India. But we are not obliged to look into ancient histories to establish the Hindu's honesty and love for truth. Go to-day into any town of India. Walk in the business section of Bombay, Calcutta, or Karachi and there you will find transactions amounting to hundreds of thousands carried on day after day without a receipt taken or given. An entry in the ledger books of both parties is all that is held necessary in such cases. In my own family, low-paid household servants drawing salaries up to a couple of hundreds a year were intrusted in the course of their duties with the handling of many thousands of dollars. And there was no least feeling of hesitation or anxiety on the part of the family, not because the servants were bonded, but because they were trusted.

A people who respect truth so highly must be lovers of learning. At every period in the history of India, a genius has been recognized and accorded assistance, even if his thesis ran contrary to the popular prejudice of the day. Whether a new sage lifted his head in the field of religion, or a thinker in the philosophical or scientific field was born, he was always allowed an opportunity to express himself under the most favorable circumstances. He did not have to fear persecution on account of his ideas. So long as he had a message to offer to mankind, he was assured an audience. *"Freedom of thought has always prevailed among all classes of people in India."*

Chivalry toward women, which has been named as another outstanding feature of Hindu character, has already been discussed in a previous chapter.

To review in detail the achievements of Hindu civilization would require volumes. India's contributions to the world's study of philosophy, science, religion, and social organization are legion. While the continent of Europe was still in a state of barbarism, the Hindus invented the sciences of grammar, arithmetic, and astronomy. They were already masters of a perfect alphabet, of a polished language, and of the most complete systems of law and social ethics that the world has ever seen. When the forefathers of the Anglo-Saxon races roamed in forests with painted bodies, the Hindus had an extensive literature, an established religion, and a developed civilization. In fact, India has ever been esteemed as the birthplace of the most natural of natural religions, as the nurse of sciences, as the inventress of fine arts, and as a fertile home for all forms of genius. Her lawgivers evolved the most wonderful fabric of social organization, and composed systems of ethics worthy of the highest praise; her philosophers invented six most profound systems of philosophy famous for their subtlety of thought and acuteness

[26] Quoted from *Sister India.*

of logic; and her religious teachers formed the two greatest religions of the world, which are to this day professed by more than half of the human race. Even in the domain of natural sciences Hindus have advanced to a high state of development, a fact which is little realized by most people. Says Sir Monier-Williams:

> "Indeed, if I may be at all allowed the anachronism, the Hindus were Spinozites more than two thousand years before the existence of Spinoza; and Darwinians many centuries before Darwin; and evolutionists many centuries before the doctrine of evolution had been accepted by the scientists of our time, and before any word like 'evolution' existed in any language of the world."

The Hindus belong to a race of mankind which has outlasted all the nations of the earth. "Before the days of Abraham India had achieved a great civilization. Other civilizations had lived and died. Egypt, Babylon, and Assyria—each came and went. After India had been flourishing for more than two thousand years, Greece appeared and passed on. The vast Roman Empire, dominating half the earth, paid huge tribute to the art and industry of India, then closed its day while the Hindu people continued to develop magnificent achievements in science, literature, art, architecture, law and government, philosophy and religion." Lord Curzon, whose judgment undoubtedly was not biased in favor of India, writes:

> "India has left a deeper mark on the history, philosophy and religion of mankind than any other terrestrial unit of the universe."

We have thus shown that as a nation the people of India have devoted their efforts more to the development of the spiritual side of life than the material. Unlike the aggressive and combative character of western civilization, the prominent features of Hindu culture are a passive and reflective attitude toward life. Compared with the record of her sister nations in the West, the history of the country has been happier, less fierce, and more peaceful and stable; the inhabitants have been more careful and thoughtful, passive and tolerant.

Two great civilizations of the world—India and China—separated only by a long border, have flourished for centuries, and not once in their entire history have they been at war with each other. They early realized the truth that the object of human life is not possession of immense wealth and dominion over weaker races for the sake of physical comforts. The aim of human effort, as they saw it, should be the development of the "mental, moral, and spiritual powers latent in man." The Hindus evolved for themselves the idea of a God that was omnipotent and all-merciful, of a human soul that was part of the Universal soul and must be pure, of a life that has the divine spark in it and must be boundless and consecrated to the service of all. Truthfulness, generosity, kindness of heart, gentleness of behavior, forgiveness, and compassion were taught in India as everyday precepts long before any such thing as ethics existed in any other part of the world. Their insistence upon kindness and charity are marks of true virtue; their belief that ethics must form the basis of religion and a moral life is the criterion of religious mind; their realization that all men are brothers and that a virtuous slave is better than a corrupt master, mark the Hindus as a race of highly intelligent and moral people.

Many of these statements may not be novel, but they have for us a significant appeal in the fact that "they were thought out and enunciated many centuries ago, and that they reflected life, not as it might be imagined in a Utopia, but as it was actually lived by the common people in the small villages and towns of India."

Thus wrote Manu, the great law-giver of India:

> "That man obtains supreme happiness hereafter who *seeks to do good to all creatures*."

CHAPTER IV

THE CASTE SYSTEM OF INDIA

The caste system of India is the most widely discussed subject all over the world; it is also the least understood. It is really surprising how little people outside of India know about the institution of caste, as it was originally evolved and perfected to form the basis of the country's social, political, and economic structure. Even students of Hindu philosophy and arts have but a very dim perception of the meaning of caste. You cannot talk about India for five minutes to any person without being confronted with the questions: "How about your caste system? Isn't it true that the upper classes refuse to marry the untouchables, and even to come into any kind of physical contact with them? Have not the Brahmans of India always lorded over the classes for their own benefit? Wouldn't they seize the power again for their own benefit if the English left India today? Don't you see that we have given freedom to the negroes in this country? They have the same political rights as white men to vote and to hold office in our government. They can come into our homes and do the cooking for us and we feel no repulsion for them. Would you permit such association of the classes in India? This equality of spirit is democracy, and until India gives up her old aristocratic habits and changes to the new democratic ideals of the age, she will never be free politically, morally, or spiritually—talk what you will of your spirituality and ethics."

I have heard such sermons over and over again from Americans of every status in life. College professors and their wives, university students, teachers, ministers, shirt dealers, insurance agents, street-car conductors, bootblacks, and railroad porters have asked me similar questions. In reply, I do not deny that one class of people is called "untouchables" and that no other class will intermingle or intermarry with them. I question most seriously, however, the truth of the premise of the second statement. Brahmans have not always ruled the country with purely selfish motives. The priestly class has wielded immense influence in India's political and social life at different periods of its history, but they have used their power mostly for the advancement of its culture and arts. To the Brahmans we owe in general the elaboration and systematization of Hindu philosophy. The vast treasures of Hindu literature and fine arts were both produced and preserved by the same class, who for unknown ages have been the sole repositories of knowledge in India. They have abused their authority at several periods, but on such occasions a great reformer like Buddha or Nanak always appeared among the Hindus and gave the corrupted priests fresh warning for their mistakes.

The power of the Brahmans was at its lowest when the British acquired India, and the Brahmans have found in the English rulers of the country great champions, who have succeeded first in demoralizing them and then in assisting them to demoralize in turn the rest of Hindu society. England with its mighty governing hand of steel is the strongest bulwark of aristocracy in India. And those who say things to the contrary either do not know the facts or they deliberately misrepresent them. We shall explain later how the subtle methods of our foreign rulers work.

Lastly, I do not deny that India needs a reorganization of its antiquated social system in order to fit properly into the modern world. Her caste regulations have given to her numerous races and classes only the negative benefits of peace and order at the expense of the positive opportunities of expansion and movement. If India is to live, and if it hopes ever to occupy its proper place among the family of nations, it must cut out of its system the cancer of untouchability. However manifest are the evils of India's rigid caste system and the necessity of its immediate overhauling, the contrast with America seems so unjust. With typical complacency, the Americans declare that there is no caste in the United States. Yet the American negro, although he has a right to vote and to hold office, has absolutely no opportunity to make use of these privileges. A child of ten has more chance of beating the world's heavyweight champion in a prize-fight than an American negro with the highest moral and educational qualifications has of becoming a governor of the smallest state in the Union. The world knows that in most states the law prohibits marriage between whites and negroes, while society everywhere will, in its own direct and emphatic American way, ban the union of a white girl to a negro. It is also true that in most states negro children are taught in separate schools, and that on Sunday colored people must go for prayer to separate churches. In the South, the center of the negro population in the United States, negroes must travel in separate carriages on railroad trains and use separate waiting rooms at the stations. It is also a matter of history that on the average more than sixty negroes are lynched in America every year by mobs for crimes, which if committed under similar conditions by white persons, would be punished through the regular course of law.

This condition in the United States does not justify the injustice of caste in India or anywhere else in the world, but it may help to give the sharp critic of the Hindu system a milder temper in his judgment by reminding him that human nature everywhere has its virtues and faults. We shall now proceed to examine the origin and the function of the caste of India.

The Sanskrit word which has been wrongly translated into caste is *Varna,* which means color. Thus the derivation of the term shows that the original classifications in Hindu society were made on the basis of color or race.[27] When the Aryans first migrated into India, they found themselves face to face with hordes of savage tribes belonging to inferior and aboriginal races. The position of those Aryan forefathers was analogous to that which later confronted the immigrants of Europe into the continents of America and Australia. While these latter invaders have sought to simplify their race problems by exterminating the original inhab-

[27] Max Müller.

itants of these countries, the early Hindus under similar conditions accepted the inferior races as units in their social structure and gave them a distinct place in the scale of labor, the nature of their functions being strictly determined according to their qualification. Even in our present stage of advancement we find that caste prevails throughout the civilized world. Its ugly symptoms are most prominent in America, Australia, and the white colonies of Africa. In the United States, the lynching of negroes in the South and the strict anti-Asiatic regulations of the state of California, and in Australia the "Keep Australia white at all cost" spirit among the population,—both of these show how deeply the spirit of race hatred has penetrated into the system of the dominant white races of the world. In the state of California, which is the center of oriental population in America, law prohibits the Asiatics (Japanese, Chinese, Hindus) from owning property and even from temporarily leasing lands for farming purposes. Another statute rules against marriage between whites and mongolians. The anti-Asiatic land lease regulations of California have given a severe blow to the oriental population of the state. The Japanese, Chinese, and Hindu immigrants to the United States were chiefly agriculturists. In the early days of California these frugal, honest, hard-working people contributed materially to the development of agriculture. And the fact cannot well be denied that the intensely hot regions of the Imperial Valley and the mosquito-ridden, swampy northern counties were brought under cultivation almost exclusively through the initiative of the Japanese and Hindu farmers of California. The Chinese, in conjunction with the other oriental races, had much to do in developing the largest asparagus growing region in the world, represented by the deltas of the Sacramento Valley. Imperial Valley is today the richest vegetable growing colony in the world. The northern counties produce the finest qualities of California rice in immense quantities, while the Delta asparagus has made California's name famous throughout the world as the producer of the choicest qualities of both white and green asparagus. But the simple, peace loving, industrious, and retiring Asiatics who toiled to make the name of agricultural California great are barred by law from making even an honest, meager living through farming on a small scale. And all because of the caste of race! As one of the state senators exclaimed not long ago: "*We must keep California safe from the yellow peril.*" To which an eminent Hindu publicist humorously replied: "I have seen no danger of a yellow peril in California except that of the 'Yellow Cabs'."

When a small group of immigrants in any land find themselves surrounded by an endless environment of barbarous tribes, we grant that the situation is critical. The small group of Aryan immigrants in India, however, unlike the American colonists, who exterminated most of the original inhabitants of the country, sought to assimilate the barbarous tribes, and hence found themselves confronted with a difficult problem. They were inspired with the desire to preserve the purity of their superior race and culture on the one hand, and to assimilate in their social system the aboriginal races as well as they could, in order to save them from annihilation. On the other hand, they felt it necessary to safeguard their race by refusing to intermarry with people on a lower scale of civilization. The Aryan forefathers of India, by giving to the original population of the country a distinct place in its social life, however low, have preserved them on the one hand from extermination and on the other from slavery of person. "Was this not the very solution which suggested itself to the American emancipator Lincoln, when at a much later date he faced the same problems under similar conditions? That adjustment of their racial differences that had been declared wise and that had been practised by the Hindus many thousand years ago, was at last acknowledged by the leaders of the western world as the only salvation from their difficult situation." In the meantime, whole populations had been obliterated, and generation after generation of human beings had been subjected to the tortures of slavery,—to injustice and suffering of the most loathsome kind.

Before we judge the Hindu too harshly for refusing to drink the same water as the non-Aryans and to eat food cooked by their hands, we must remember that most of the aborigines of India were carrion eaters and were more unclean than their Aryan neighbors. The Aryan would not perform any act of life without previously taking his morning bath; he was scrupulously clean in all his habits. He felt, therefore, that it was merely a hygienic precaution not to allow the filthy barbarians access to his person or his house. But it is the nature of caste to convert temporary inhibitions into permanent barriers. In so far as the early Hindu sociologists safeguarded the superior Aryan culture by laying down strict rules—such as the refusals to intermarry and to drink the same water—,they were in the right. Therein they recognized the diversity of races and the necessity of keeping separate the most highly developed and the least civilized. "But they erred most dangerously in not grasping the fact that differences between human beings are not fixed like the physical barriers of mountains, but are mutable and fluid with life's flow."[28] "It is the law of life to change its shape and volume through the impact of environment." "Was it not expected that contact with the civilized Aryans would develop among the aboriginal inhabitants of India the wholesome qualities of cleanliness, honesty, peace, and love characteristic of an advanced race?"[29] To have thus bound in an iron frame the growing body of a healthy people was not only an intellectual blunder, but a spiritual crime. As a result, India, which is fundamentally one nation, is now torn into innumerable castes and communities. And this is the cause of her degradation and ruin. India, which should be the mightiest nation of the world today, on account of her ancient culture and history and the nobility and height of her spiritual idealism, is now fallen. If there exists anywhere the law of Karma, the Hindus of the present age are atoning for the sins of omission of their ancient forefathers. The great, great, great grandchildren of those who denied their fellow humans the natural rights of humanity have been cast out of the world's progressive life as the black pariahs of the race. In a recent decision of the United States Supreme Court, which has ruled out the natives of India as ineligible to the citizenship of America, the Honorable Justice remarked: "Hindus of the high caste belonging to the Aryan or Caucasian race, are not white persons." Those Hindus who pride themselves as *twice-born Brahmans* should take notice of this language.

Let those who wish clamor loud about their Nordic superiority or Brahmanic purity. What is needed in the world today is not the purity of the race so much as

[28] Tagore.
[29] Tagore.

the purity of the human soul and its motives. How far the soul of the western people is clean I would not say, but being myself a Hindu, I do know that the soul of India is black. By denying to their fellow brethren their rightful position as human beings, the upper classes of India have sinned most atrociously against themselves and their gods. "Where the touch from a fellow human being pollutes and his shadow corrupts, there the gods can never reside, or truth prevail." The laws of nature are immutable. You may err against them for a short time, but you cannot afford to ignore their existence forever. In the ultimate reckoning nature will fall upon you in a mad fury and wreak for your mistakes a terrible vengeance. Thus, those who set out to humble and degrade others are in turn humbled themselves. "In the act of tyranny, the tyrant loses sight of his ideals and develops the pride of power, which is another name for the lowering of his soul. Like a man under the influence of liquor, he may feel for the time powerful and strong; yet from the moment an individual loses hold of truth, the insanity of cruelty and injustice starts its deadly work, which will end in his ruin and death."[30]

If the Hindus wish to survive, they must first humble themselves before the members of the lower classes against whom they have long sinned so terribly. They must purify their souls and promise to sin no more. Unless they can do this, it is foolish to expect national freedom, and it is idle to desire it. Those who will not grant freedom to those below them, are themselves not fitted to have freedom.

The high-born Hindu should think over the situation in which he finds himself today. When he despises the Mohammedans and the lower caste Hindus to such an extent that the mere physical touch from the most highly cultured and clean of their kind will spoil the cooking of the wretchedest of the so-called high-caste, how in the name of God, man, or the devil can he expect them to love and serve him? The entire history of mankind does not afford one instance in which an oppressed class has fought to protect the honor or power of its oppressors. It is idle to hope that the oppressed classes of India will ever consent to shed their life-blood to win the freedom of their country. They may at some time make immense sacrifices in the service and at the bidding of such a universal soul as Gandhi, or perhaps unite to drive out an intensely hated foreigner like the British. True liberation, however, can be brought to the nation only through the spiritual unity of its peoples; under the present social regulations the hope of such a union is not only visionary but idiotic.

My misguided Hindu brethren of India should remember what the followers of Nanak, the Sikhs, have already done, and what the Arya Samajists are doing now in the Punjab. They can do the same and much more! If they need a leader to guide them, they can find no one holier or wiser in the whole world today than Mahatma Gandhi, who will show them the light as soon as they are ready to see it. Gandhi, the Mahatma (the Great Soul), the leader of millions, has adopted an untouchable girl into his family, whom Mrs. Gandhi is bringing up with their own children in their home. This action has made Gandhi no smaller in the sight of God or man. Will it make other Hindus smaller if they come forward and say to their brethren: "Come, brothers, we embrace you. We shall forget the past and be one

[30] Tagore.

again. Children of the same Father, we are all equal before His law. There shall be, in future, no high or low among us. Brahman and Sudra, Mohammedan and Parsi, we shall join hands and strive to bring our motherland back to its former vigor." Then and then alone will the regeneration of India be possible.

We find that quite early in the country's history Hindu society fell into two main divisions, the Aryans and the non-Aryans. The former were again divided into three orders represented by priests, warriors, and Aryan farmers or merchants; while the non-Aryans constituted the servant class or the Sudras. The division of society into the three priestly, warrior, and merchant classes is a natural one. We find its parallel in ancient Persia, where the division of the community into priests, warriors, and husbandmen is shown in the Avesta. "In fact, the caste sentiment prevails in greater or less degree in all monarchical countries of the world. In mediæval Europe the sentiment of caste grew so strong that it found expression in literature and law."

The work of society in India was distributed among the four castes as follows:

1. Brahmans, the priestly class, were the teachers of the rest of mankind. Their function was to study the Vedic scriptures and various branches of knowledge such as science and philosophy. They were to offer spiritual guidance and to assist all other classes in the performance of religious rites and ceremonies. Everyone depended upon them for favor with the gods, for they were believed to be specially favored to interpret the Veda. As a tribute to the Brahmans' spirituality and learning, they were respected and loved by the other classes. Their simple physical needs were amply provided for, so that they were absolutely free from any form of material care. Within the realm of their appointed duties they were the free, intellectual lords of the Universe. This rule applied to the entire class of scholars and religious teachers, and not to any chosen group among them. A parallel state of intellectual freedom could be reached in the modern western world if *all* of its professors and religious instructors were born with independent means. The Brahmans' threefold function of teaching, studying, and renunciation inspired among the masses of mankind the feelings of reverence and affection for them. "A Brahman's body was on that account regarded as sacred, and to hurt him in any way was the heaviest sin; while to kill a Brahman was an unpardonable sin which could not be expiated even by penance through an unlimited number of successive rebirths."

While the priestly class thus received the love and homage of the populace, they at the same time enjoyed many immunities and exemptions. From certain punishments a Brahman was always exempt, and his high rank secured him pardon for numerous crimes. On the other hand, special rules were laid down for his class in order to preserve its sanctity. "He could never drink, eat meat, or enjoy the coarser pleasures of life." In fact, the law codes of the different castes specify that for certain offences a Brahman should be punished many times more than a man belonging to the lower classes. This severity was due to the belief of the law-givers of India that "greater knowledge demanded greater restraint, and that with the raise in a person's status his responsibility must also rise." The rule for a Brahman as given by Vasistha is this: "Those are true Brahmans who, well-taught, have subdued their passions, injure no living being, and close their fingers when gifts are offered them." Again, the same teacher has said that a Brahman by birth is not a true Brahman but a slave unless he lives a virtuous and clean life devoted to study and restraint. Says Manu, the great law-giver of India: "A Brahman who does not live as a Brahman is no better than a slave." He could be made an outcast and demoted socially into a lower rank.

Thus we find that while on the one hand their higher status won for the Brahmans respect and reverence from the populace, on the other hand their better position imposed upon them special restraints. It is difficult for us to realize the wisdom of this dictum, yet the Hindu law which prohibited its intellectual classes from possessing property and otherwise amassing wealth was one of the most profoundly wise laws in the social history of man. Looked at in conjunction with the text "that a householder obtains high merit in this life and hereafter by giving food, drink, and raiment to Brahmans," the dictum against the acquiring of wealth by the Brahman class will appear not only wise but highly just. "Here was a class of scholars, leaders of mankind, who were safe from the two great evils which are the curse of their noble profession—the anxiety of making a livelihood and the temptation to acquire fortunes."

Lest it be supposed that the scholars of India lived on the charity of other classes, a condition which is not regarded in the West as honorable, it may be added here in the form of a corollary that charity in India has an altogether different meaning from that in the West. The motives behind such acts in India and the western countries are quite different. According to Hindu theology, the giver of a gift and not the recipient is the beneficiary. Absolutely no sense of pride or self-importance is attached to the bestowing of gifts. Such deeds are always accompanied by a sense of deep humility and thankfulness in the heart of the householder. "It is the *dharma*, which may be translated as the *man-ness of man*, of every householder to provide handsomely for the needs of a Brahman, and he does this from a sense of religious and social duty as well as from a desire for a religious blessing." It is as much the householder's duty and joy in life to accommodate a Brahman as it is the hope and delight of every mother to comfort her child. To assist a strange scholar in his work is considered no more an act of charity in India than is the support of a son at college in Europe or America. The experiences of Mrs. Margaret E. Noble, an Englishwoman of literary eminence, who went to India for a study of its philosophy, are illustrative of the Hindu psychology in this matter. She relates in her book *The Web of Indian Life* the story of her residence in the Hindu section of Calcutta. After news reached the neighborhood that she had come to India as a student, she found in front of her door one morning a jar of fresh milk and a basket of provisions left by some unknown visitor. This experience was repeated almost every day of the year until her departure. Yet the donors of these simple presents never made themselves known to Mrs. Noble, nor was she ever questioned by anyone of her neighbors regarding her views on Hindu life. They did not care whether she was friendly or hostile to them in her judgments. The fact that she had come among them as a *student* was sufficient reason for them to provide for her. *India is the only country in the world where poets and priests never starve.*

2. *Khashatriyas* or the royal and military class were the rulers of the country, and their duty was to protect the other classes. The Khashatriyas constituted the knightly caste of India. They were brave and chivalrous. The enjoyment of the senses and of pleasures subject to such laws as may protect the weak from the strong were the legitimate rewards of this class. Many a deed of extreme heroism committed by this class under the noble impulse to protect justice or to serve Cupid is related in the epic history of India.

"Chivalry taught them the lessons of gaiety and enjoyment. They learned to admire and desire beauty. Unlike the austere ascetic Brahmans, passion and pleasure in the company of woman was sought by the gallant suitors of the warrior class. Women were often objects of jealousy, and they always exercised great power through their beauty and charm. Fine, full-blooded creatures they were, who knew how to get and give love. Both men and women loved superbly and passionately. Their passions were strong and consuming and their thirst for love great." Theirs was a love about which a poet sung:

"Give me your love for a day,
A night, an hour;
If the wages of sin are death,
I am willing to pay.

Oh! Aziza, whom I adore,
Aziza, my one delight,
Only one night—I will die before day,
And trouble your life no more."

(LAWRENCE HOPE.)[31]

3. The *Vaishya* or the merchant and husbandman class constituted the body of the people. Theoretically they were the equals of the other classes of the Aryan family; but "practically this class together with the fourth caste, namely the Sudras, formed the majority of the population, whose duty it was to support and serve the two upper classes." They managed the business life of the country and were responsible for the maintenance of the other classes. They tilled the soil and managed the entire commercial and industrial affairs of the land. This class was again subdivided into various groups according to their profession. This classification of the middle class of India on the basis of occupation was founded upon a thorough understanding of the laws of heredity—"the purpose being to develop the best qualities through heredity transmission. Thereby an attempt was made to develop further the brain of the scholar, the skill of the craftsman, and the ingenuity of the trader through the cumulative influence of careful selection from generation to generation." By thus shutting different trades and professions into air-tight compartments the Vaishya deprived themselves of the benefits of the infusion of young blood into the old system. While on the one hand it had the wholesome effect of reducing the evils of competition to the minimum, on the other it has gradually tended "to turn arts into crafts and genius into skill."

4. *Sudras* or the servant class constituted the entire aboriginal non-Aryan pop-

[31] Quoted from Otto Rothfield—*Women of India.*

ulation of the country, whose function was to do mechanical service in the household life of the community. According to Manu the highest merit for this class was to serve faithfully the other three classes. The Sudras performed the most degrading tasks, and were allowed to come into contact with the Aryan population only as menials. On account of their filthy habits these aboriginals were not allowed a close approach to the persons of the higher classes—hence the origin of the term "untouchable." Yet the fact stands that even the "untouchables" are members of the Hindu family group. At marriages and other festivals gifts are freely exchanged between them and the upper classes. For a householder it is equally important to participate in the ceremonies of the village "untouchables" and his own cousins. I remember very clearly how as a young boy I was instructed by my mother to bow each morning before every elder member of the family, nor forgetting the servants, or Sudras.

Bhagavad Gita, the Bible of the Hindus, lays down the following rules for the different castes of India:

> "The duties of the Brahmins, Kshatriyas, Vaishyas, as also of Sudras, are divided in accordance with their nature-born qualities. Peace, self-restraint, austerities, purity, forgiveness, and uprightness, knowledge, direct intuition, and faith in God are the natural qualities of the Brahmin. Of the Kshatriyas, bravery, energy, fortitude, dexterity, fleeing not in battle, gift and lordliness are the nature-born qualities. Agriculture, protection of cows, merchandise, and various industries are the nature-born duties of the Vaishyas. Conscientiousness in menial service is the nature-born duty of the Sudras. A man attains perfection by performing those duties which he is able to do."

This division of duties among the different castes "in accordance with their nature-born qualities" needs special notice. We find here that the original distinctions between different classes were made on the basis of their natural qualifications. "The purpose of the early Hindu sociologists was to design a society in which opportunity was allowed to everyone for only such experience as his mental and spiritual status was capable." In the beginning, castes were not fixed by iron barriers, nor were the occupations and professions of the people hereditary. There was freedom for expansion, and everyone enjoyed the privilege of rising into the higher scales of social rank through a demonstration of his power and ability to do so. It is a curious fact of Hindu history that nearly all of its incarnations,—namely, Buddha, Rama, Krishna—belonged to the second or military caste. But the Hindu castes had already lost their flexible natures as early as the sixth century B.C., when Buddha once again preached the doctrines of equality to all classes of people. Through the influence of Buddhist teachings and for over a thousand years during which Buddhism reigned over India, artificial hereditary caste divisions among peoples were almost entirely demolished and forgotten. "Buddha gave to the spirit of caste a death-blow. He refused to admit differences between persons because of their color or race. He would not recognize a Brahman because he was born a Brahman. On the other hand he distinguished between people according to their intellectual status and moral worth."[32] He who possessed the qualities of "peace, self-restraint, self-control, righteousness, devotion, love for humanity, and divine wisdom" was alone a true Brahman. To the Buddhist, caste was less important than character. His Jataka tales preached this doctrine in a simple but highly eloquent manner:

"It is not right
To call men white
Who virtue lack;
For it is sin
And not the skin
That makes men black.
Not by the cut of his hair,
Not by his clan or birth,
May a Brahmin claim the Brahmin's name,
But only by moral worth."[33]

About 600 A. D. however, when Buddhism declined and the Brahmans regained their power, caste was once again established on the old hereditary lines. Since that time the influence of the vicious system has prevailed, except when it was checked by such teachers as Chaityna who have regularly appeared at critical periods of the country's history. Nanak's influence in modern times has been the strongest in breaking down the barriers of caste. He was born near Lahore (Punjab) in the year 1469 A.D. and became the founder of the Sikh religion. He recognized the equality of all human beings, irrespective of their color, rank, or sex. In one of his most popular verses he says:

> "One God produced the light, and all creatures are of His creation. When the entire universe has originated from one source, why do men call one good and the other bad?"

Even in the present day the followers of Nanak are a tremendous force in demolishing caste. In a recent general assembly of the Sikhs held at Amritsar (the official headquarters of the Sikh religion) it was announced that at all future gatherings of the community, and in all of its free kitchens everywhere, cooks belonging to the "untouchable" class shall be freely employed and even given special preference. As a beginning of this policy the usual pudding offering of the Sikhs was distributed by "untouchable" men and women to a group of nearly twenty thousand delegates at the convention. Prior to this, resolutions condemning "untouchability" had been passed on innumerable occasions at social service conferences; but never before had the ages-old custom been trampled upon, in a practical way, by any other community belonging to the Hindu religion. May this auspicious beginning inaugurate a triumphant conclusion. It is sincerely hoped that the leadership of Gandhi and the virile followers of Nanak in removing the curse of "untouchability" will soon be recognized by the entire Hindu community. This alone could insure the enthusiastic Hindu nationalists political economic freedom for their country. Had it not been for the selfishness of the Brahmans during the mediæval

[32] E. W. Hopkins.

[33] Jataka, 440. Quoted from E. W. Hopkins *Ethics of India.*

period,—a selfishness which has tended to segregate the Hindus into different sections through the strict caste restrictions of various types,—India would occupy today the vanguard of the world's progress instead of the rear. In spite of her present weakness India possesses, however, within herself a marvelous reserve force which will enable her to pass through this crisis. While the haughty West, which has always delighted in taunting the Hindus for the latter's caste, has not even begun to examine her problem of race-conflict, India is already on its way to solving her own caste problem. Gradually, as the younger generation among the Hindus gains more power, "untouchability" and its allied diseases will disappear. Personally, I believe that the leaders of India are headed in the right direction, and that soon equality among members of the different castes will be established in the country as a permanent part of its social structure.

"In the Hindu system, once the people were divided into different castes, equality of opportunity for all prevailed within their own castes, while the caste or group as a whole had collective responsibilities and privileges." Each caste had its own rules and code of honor; and so long as a man's mode of living was acceptable to his caste-fellows, the rest of the community did not care about it at all. On the other hand, a man's status in the outside world or his wealth made no change in his rank within the caste. I shall offer an illustration from my own experience. During the mourning week after the death of a near relative of His Royal Highness, the ruling Prince of the native State of Kashmir, Her Royal Highness gave a state reception to the sympathizing friends. Whereas she greeted the wives of the two highest officials in the State, the English Resident and the Prime Minister, with a nod of the head from her seat, Her Royal Highness had to receive standing the humble housekeeper in my brother's home, because the latter belonged to the same caste as the ruling prince. "Society thus organized can be best described by the term Guild Socialism."

Another distinctive feature in the study of its caste is the communal character of Hindu life. Hindu society was established on a basis of group morality. No set of rules were held binding on all classes alike, but within a given caste the freedom of the individual was subordinated to the interest of the caste. Men lived not for their own interests or comfort, but for the benefit of the community. It was a life of self-sacrifice, and the concept of duty was paramount. The good of caste, of race, of nation stood first, and that of the individual second. Social welfare was placed before the happiness of the individual. "For the family sacrifice the individual, for the community the family, for the country the community, for the soul all the world."

Which of the two ideals, the communism of the Hindu or the individualism of the Westerner is the better? Says Rabindranath Tagore: "Europe may have preached and striven for individualism, but where else in the world is the individual so much of slave?"

On the other hand it must be remembered also that all ideals are good only so far as they assist the individual to develop his full manhood, and the moment they begin to hamper him in his natural growth and thwart his own will they lose their value. So long as the caste regulations of the Hindus assisted them in their spiritual development, they were justified. But the moment they began to lose their original character and became an oppression in the hands of the priestly classes, who used their authority to stifle the nation's spirit, they had lost their usefulness and invited the ridicule and censure of all intelligent thinkers.

Where finer feelings of fraternal human-fellowship prevailed over self-interest and individual gain, in such a community no voice cried in vain at the time of distress. When deaths in the family left small children parentless, or sickness and misfortunes made homes penniless, the protection of other members of the caste was always available for those in need. Orphans and helpless members within the caste were taken into the homes of caste brothers and carefully brought up and fed with the rest as members of the family. Here the lucky and the unlucky were brought up side by side. Thus there has never arisen in India the necessity of orphanages and poorhouses. As was said by an eminent English writer:[34] "For to the ripe and mellow genius of the East it has been always clear that the defenceless and unfortunate require a *home*, not a barrack."

Let us now review the entire subject of caste thus: The Aryan invaders of India found themselves surrounded by hordes of aboriginal and inferior races. Under similar conditions the European invaders of America and Australia exterminated the original population by killing them off, or converted them into human slaves; the Hindu Aryans avoided both of these inhumanities by taking the native inhabitants of the land into their social life. They gave these inferior peoples a distinct place in the scale of labor, and assigned to them the duties of menial service, for which alone they were qualified at the time. Further, to safeguard their superior culture, the Aryan leaders laid down strict rules against intermarriage with their non-Aryan neighbors. And as these aboriginals were filthy in their habits and mostly carrion-eaters, it was also ordained as a measure of hygienic precaution that the Aryans should not be allowed to drink the same water or eat food cooked by non-Aryan hands. This was the beginning of untouchability.

Simultaneously with this racial division rose a functional division among the Aryan population separating it into three orders of priests, warriors, and husbandmen. This constituted the four-fold division of the Hindu caste system—the Aryan inhabitants of the land forming the first three castes of Brahmans, Khashatriyas, and Vaishyas, while the non-Aryans constituted the fourth caste of servants or Sudras. At first these divisions into different castes were flexible and persons in the lower castes were allowed to rise into the ones higher by virtue of their merit. We find that most of the historic religious teachers of the Hindus, namely, Rama, Krishna, and Buddha, came from the second class.

Gradually, however, the castes began to lose their flexible nature, and before the birth of Buddha in the year 600 B. C. they had already acquired a hereditary character. The teachings of Buddhism had the tendency to break down the hereditary barriers of caste, and during a thousand years of its reign the people of India had forgotten their caste boundaries. "Around 600 A. D. Buddhism began to decline and the Brahman priests gained fresh prestige. They set up the different castes on the old hereditary lines once again, and, except for a few local breaks

[34] Margaret E. Noble.

through the appearance of such leaders as Nanak in Punjab and Chaityna in the South, the spirit of caste has prevailed throughout Hindu India since the decline of Buddhism." The greatest champion of the lower classes who has appeared in recent times is the peaceful leader of India's silent revolution, Mahatma Gandhi. He has spoken and written against untouchability and its allied evils more bitterly and longer than against other vital political and economic wrongs of the country. He has told his countrymen time and again that India's soul cannot become pure so long as untouchability stays amongst the Hindus to defile it. And as a proof of his own sincerity in the matter he has adopted in his own family an untouchable girl whom he calls the joy of the household.

The evils of caste are quite manifest. It has tended to divide the Hindu community into various groups and thus destroyed among them unity of feeling which alone could insure national strength. Lack of united power opened the way for foreign invasions, which, again, has resulted in dragging India down from her former place of glory to her present state of humiliation and ruin. Yet alongside with the many evils of India's caste system several advantages have accrued from it. Its existence has tended to make the people of India conservative and tolerant. With the institution of caste they felt so well fortified within themselves that they did not fear the influx of new ideas into their midst. India offered a safe and welcome home to the oppressed minorities from other lands. The Parsis and Jews came and settled there. They were not merely tolerated but welcomed by the Hindus, because the latter, assured of their own wonderful powers of resistance, had nothing to fear from outside influences. The Hindu caste system may be described as "the social formulation of defence minus all elements of aggression." Since the beginning of her history India has been subjected to numerous invasions, but she has stood against them successfully. In the cultural sense India, instead of being conquered, "has always succeeded in conquering her conquerors." The invaders belonging to different civilizations and races have come and disappeared, one after the other; but India still survives.[35]

Again, in the Hindus' scheme of the division of labor care was taken to assign to every man his task and remuneration in such a manner as to avoid all unnecessary friction among the different classes. Its value will be readily recognized by those who are familiar with the evils of modern industrialism, arising from the intense hatred within the different classes.

Finally, it must be said to the credit of Hindu sociologists that, at least, they had the courage to face the problem of race-conflict with a sympathetic mind. The problem was not of their creation. The diversity of races existed in India before these new Aryan invaders came into the country. The caste system of the Hindus was the result of their sincere endeavors to seek a solution of their difficult problem. Its object was to keep the different races together and yet afford each one of them opportunity to express itself in its own separate way. "India may not have achieved complete success in this. But who else has? It was, at least, better than the best which the West has thought of so far. There the stronger races have either exterminated the weaker ones like the Red Indians in America, or shut them out

[35] Tagore.

completely like the Asiatics in Australia and America." "Whatever may be its merits," says Tagore, "you will have to admit that it does not spring from the higher impulses of civilization, but from the lower passions of greed and hatred."

CHAPTER V

GANDHI—THE MAN AND HIS MESSAGE

Mohandass Karamchand Gandhi is today the acknowledged leader of three hundred million inhabitants of India. He is the author of the Non-violent Non-coöperation movement, adopted by the Indian National Congress as a weapon of passive resistance wherewith to win India's freedom. In March, 1922, because of his public activities in India as a leader of this movement, Gandhi was convicted on the charge of promoting disaffection towards the British crown, and was sentenced to six years' incarceration. He was released from prison, however, in 1924 by a special order of the British Labor Government. Since that time he has remained the most powerful and beloved public figure in the nationalist movement of India.

His movement has aroused great interest among the different peoples of the world. But the information given to the outside public has been so vague and disconnected that it has led to very erroneous conclusions. So much of pure nonsense in the form of praise and ridicule of Gandhi and his activities has been passed around that it has become difficult for the earnest student to separate the real from the fictitious. Therefore it is only fitting that we should make a careful study of the man and his message.

A sufficient number of scholars, students, missionaries, travelers, and writers have studied him carefully enough to enable them to form a reliable opinion. Irrespective of their missions, opinions, and designations, these investigators all agree as to the magnetic personality of Gandhi and to the purity of his private and public life. "His sweet, subtle sense of humor, and his profound confidence in the ultimate triumph of truth and justice as against falsehood and oppression never fail to influence and inspire everyone who comes his way." Even the very judge who, seven years ago, sentenced him to six years' incarceration could not resist the temptation to call him "a great patriot and a great leader," and to pay him the tribute: "Even those who differ from you in politics look up to you as a man of high ideals and as leading a noble and even saintly life."

Gandhi, born at Ahmedabad (India) in October, 1869, had all the advantages of an early education under careful guidance. His father, Karamchand Gandhi, a wealthy man and a statesman by profession, combined in himself the highest political wisdom and learning together with an utter simplicity of manner. He was respected throughout Deccan, in which (province) he was prime minister of a native state, as a just man and an uncompromising champion of the weak. "Gandhi's mother was an orthodox Hindu lady, with stubborn religious conceptions. She led a very simple and dignified life after the teachings of the Hindu Vedas." She was a very jealous and affectionate mother and took a deep interest in the bringing up of her children. Gandhi, the favorite "Mohan" of his parents, was the center of all the cares and discipline of his loving relatives. He inherited from his father a determination of purpose and the tenacity of a powerful will, and from his mother a sense of religious and moral purity of life. After graduating from a native school in his home town, he was sent to England to finish his education. He fitted himself for the bar at the University of London, and on his return to India was admitted as an advocate of the High Court of Bombay. While still in London, Gandhi acquired the habit of passing the best part of his days in solitude. From the temptations of the boisterous London life he could find escape only when he sat alone by his window, violin in his lap, and thought of an unconquered spiritual world in his mind. A product of the early favorable circumstances and all the advanced education, Gandhi is thus a highly cultured gentleman with finished manners. He possesses a happy temperament with but a tinge of melancholy pervading his life and conduct.

As a patriot and leader of an oppressed people struggling for freedom, Gandhi belongs in the category of the world's great liberators with such men as Washington, Lincoln, and Mazzini. As a saintly person who has dedicated his life to preaching the gospel of love and truth, and who has actually lived up to his preachings, he ranks among such of the world's great sages as Buddha, Jesus, and Socrates. On the one hand a dangerous political agitator, an untiring and unresting promoter of a huge mass revolution; yet on the other an uncompromising champion of non-violence, a saint with the motto, "Love thine enemies," Gandhi stands unique, supreme, unequalled, and unsurpassed.

His theory of a non-violent mass revolution aiming at the dethronement of a powerful, militaristic government like the British Bureaucracy in India, though strange and impractical at first thought, is yet very simple and straightforward.

"Man is born free, and yet," lamented Rousseau, "he is everywhere in chains." "Man is born free, why should he refuse to live free?" questions Gandhi. Freedom is man's birthright. With unlimited liberty in thought and action man could live in perfect peace and harmony on condition that all men would rigidly observe their own duties and keep within their own rights. "But men as they are and not as they should be, possess a certain amount of animal nature. In some it is subdued, while in others, let loose, it becomes the cause of disturbance and dislocates all freedom." To safeguard against the encroachment of such natures on the "natural rights" and privileges of others, men have organized themselves into groups called states. "By so doing, each voluntary member of this state foregoes some of his personal rights in exchange for certain individual privileges and communal rights to be secured under its protection. The government of a country is thus a matter of voluntary choice by its people and is organized to carry on such functions as shall conduce to the highest good of the maximum number." When it becomes corrupt, when instead of protecting its members from every form of evil and disorder, it becomes an instrument of the forces of darkness and a tool of corruption, citizens have an inalienable right to demand a change in the existing order. They might first attempt peaceful reform, but should such attempts come to nought, the right of revolution is theirs. It is indeed their right to refuse their coöperation, direct or indirect, with a government which has been responsible for the spiritual decadence and political degeneracy of their country. Gandhi explains his attitude thus:

> "We must refuse to wait for the wrong to be righted till the wrong-doer has been roused to a sense of his iniquity. We must not, for fear of ourselves or others having to suffer, remain participators in it. But we must combat the wrong by ceasing to assist the wrong-doer directly or indirectly.
>
> "If a father does an injustice, it is the duty of his children to leave the parental roof. If the head-master of a school conducts his institution on an immoral basis, the pupils must leave school. If the chairman of a corporation is corrupt, the members must wash their hands clean of his corruption by withdrawing from it; even so, if a government does a grave injustice, the subject must withdraw coöperation, wholly or partially, sufficiently to wean the ruler from his wickedness. In each of the cases conceived by me, there is an element of suffering whether mental or physical. Without such suffering, it is impossible to attain freedom."
>
> * * * * *
>
> "The business of every god-fearing person is to dissociate himself from evil in total disregard of consequences. He must have faith in a good deed producing only a good result; that in my opinion is the Gita doctrine of work without attachment. God does not permit him to peep into the future. He follows truth although the following of it may endanger his very life. He knows that it is better to die in the way of God than to live in the way of Satan. Therefore whoever is satisfied that this Government represents the activity of Satan has no choice left to him but to dissociate himself from it...."

For a period of more than twenty-five years, Gandhi coöperated with the British Empire whenever it was threatened and stood in need. Though he vehemently criticized it when it went wrong, yet he did not wish its destruction until his final decision of non-coöperation in 1920. "He felt, that in spite of its abuses and shortcomings, the system was mainly and intrinsically good." Gandhi joined in the World War on the side of the Allies. When the war started, he was in England, where he organized an Ambulance Corps from among the group of his compatriots residing there. Later on, in India, he accepted a position in the British Recruiting Service as an honorary officer, and strained himself to the breaking point in his efforts to assist Great Britain.

"Gandhi gave proofs of his loyalty to the Empire and of his faith in British justice by valuable services also on the occasion of the Anglo-Boer war (1899) and the Zulu revolt (1906). In recognition of his services on the two latter occasions he was awarded gold medals, and his name was each time mentioned in the dispatches. Later, on his return to India, he was awarded the Kaiser-i-Hind Gold Medal by Lord Hardinge in recognition of his humanitarian services in South Africa." These medals he determinedly, though regretfully, returned to the Viceroy of India on August 1, 1920. The letter that accompanied them besides other things contained this statement:

> "Your Excellency's light-hearted treatment of the official crime, your exoneration of Sir Michael O'Dwyer, Mr. Montague's dispatch and above all the shameful ignorance of the Punjab events and callous disregard of the feelings of Indians betrayed by the House of Lords, have filled me with the gravest misgivings regarding the future of the Empire, have estranged me completely from the present Government and have disabled me from tendering, as I have hitherto whole-heartedly tendered, my loyal coöperation."

His statement in court at the time of his conviction in March, 1922, when he pleaded guilty, reads:

> "From a staunch loyalist and coöperator, I have become an uncompromising disaffectionist and non-coöperator.... To preach disaffection towards the existing system of government has became almost a passion with me.... If I were set free, I would still do the same. I would be failing in my duty if I did not do so.... I had to submit to a system which has done irreparable harm to my country, or to incur the mad fury of my people, bursting forth when they heard the truth from my lips.... I do not ask for mercy. I am here to invite and to submit to the highest penalty that can be inflicted upon me for what in law is a crime, but which is the first duty of every citizen.... Affection cannot be manufactured or regulated by law.... I hold it to be a virtue to be disaffected towards a government which, in its totality, has done more harm to India than any previous system.... It is the physical and brutal ill-treatment of humanity which has made many of my co-workers and myself impatient of life itself."

The chief distinction between Gandhi and other liberators, the chief difference between him and other leaders was that he wanted his countrymen to love their friends, and yet not to hate their enemies. "Hatred ceaseth not by hatred; hatred ceaseth by love" was his sole plea to his fellowmen. He enjoined them to love their oppressors, for through love and suffering alone could these same oppressors be brought to see their mistakes. Thus, following his public announcement of the non-coöperation policy he embarked upon an extensive tour of the country. Wherever he went he preached disaffection towards the existing government.

Gandhi's whole political career is inspired by a deep love for his suffering countrymen. His heart burns with the desire to free his country from its present state of thraldom and helpless servitude. India, the cradle of civilization and culture, for ages the solitary source of light and of wisdom, whence issued the undying message of Buddhist missionaries, where empires flourished under the careful guidance of distinguished statesmen, the land of Asoka and Akbar, lies to-day at the tender mercy of a haughty conqueror, intoxicated and maddened by the conquest of a helpless people. "Her arts degenerated, her literatures dead, her beautiful industries perished, her valor done," she presents but a pitiful picture to the onlooking world. Gandhi, the heroically determined son of India, feels the impulse to save his motherland from the present state of "slow torture, emasculation, and degradation," and suggests to his countrymen the use of the unique yet powerful weapon of peaceful non-coöperation. Through this slow process of "self-denial" and "self-purification" he proposes to carry his country forward till the goal of its political emancipation and its spiritual freedom is fully realized. Political freedom might be secured by force, but that is not what Gandhi wishes. Unsatisfied with mere freedom of the body, he soars higher and strives for a sublimer form of liberty, the freedom of the soul. To the question, "Shall India follow the stern example of Europe, and fight out its struggle for political and economic independence?" Gandhi replies with an emphatic and unqualified "No." "What has Europe's powerful military and material organization done to insure its future peace?" Romain Rolland answers: "Half a century ago might dominated right. To-day things are far worse. Might is right. Might has devoured right."

No people, no nation has ever won or ever can win real freedom through violence. "Violence implies the use of force, and the force is oppressive. Those who fight and win with force, ultimately find it both convenient and expedient to follow the line of least resistance; and they continue to rely upon force in time of peace as well, ostensibly to maintain law and order, but practically to suppress and stifle every rising spirit. The power may thus change hands, yet leave the evil process to continue without a moment's break. Non-violence does not carry with it this degeneration which is inherent in the use of violence." Gandhi is highly eloquent on this score when he says:

> "They may forget non-coöperation, but they dare not forget non-violence. Indeed, non-coöperation is non-violence. We are violent when we support a government whose creed is violence. It bases itself finally not on right but might. Its last appeal is not to reason, nor the heart, but to the sword. We are tired of this creed and we have risen against it. Let us ourselves not belie our profession by being violent."

"One must love one's enemies while hating their deeds; hate Satanism while loving Satan" is the principal article of Gandhi's faith, and he has proved himself worthy of this lofty profession by his own personal conduct. Through all the stormy years of his life he has stood firm in his noble convictions, with his love untainted, his faith unchallenged, his veracity unquestioned, and his courage undaunted. "No criticism however sharp, no abuse however bitter, ever affected the loving heart of Gandhi." In the knowledge of his life-long political associates (members of the Indian National Congress and of other such organizations), Gandhi has never, even in moments of the most violent excitement, lost control of himself. When light-hearted criticisms have been showered on his program by younger and more inexperienced colleagues, when the bitterest sarcasms have been aimed at him by older associates, he has never revealed by so much as a tone of his voice the slightest touch of anger or the slightest show of contempt. *His limit of tolerance has not yet been reached.*

During the last ten years of his political life in India when he guided the destines of his countrymen as leader of a great movement, Gandhi again gave unmistakable proofs of the vastness of his love for mankind. That his love is not reserved for his compatriots alone, but extends even to his bitterest enemies, he revealed clearly throughout the most critical period of his life. His enemies, the British bureaucrats, tried to nip his movement in the very bud by using all the power at their command to discredit him in the eyes of his countrymen and of the world outside. Calumnies were heaped upon him from all sides. He was called a "hypocrite," an "unscrupulous agitator," a "disguised autocrat." The vast number of his followers were branded as "dumb-cattle," and hundreds of thousands of them were flogged, imprisoned, and in some cases even shot for no other offense than that of wearing the coarse hand-spun "Gandhi cap" and singing the Indian national hymn. Even in such trying moments he remained firm in his faith, and loyal to his professions. Evidence as to the undisturbed, peaceful condition of his mind and spirit is amply furnished by the following statements which he gave to the Indian press in those turbulent days:

> "Our non-violence teaches us to love our enemies. By non-violent non-coöperation we seek to conquer the wrath of English administrators and their supporters. We must love them and pray to God that they might have wisdom to see what appears to us to be their error. It must be the prayer of the strong and not of the weak. In our strength must we humble ourselves before our maker.
>
> "In the moment of our trial and our triumph let me declare my faith. I believe in loving my enemies.... I believe in the power of suffering to melt the stoniest heart.... We must by our conduct demonstrate to every Englishman that he is as safe in the remotest corner of India as he professes to feel behind the machine gun."
>
> * * * * *
>
> "There is only one God for us all, whether we find him through the Bible, the Koran, the Gita, the Zindvesta or the Talmud, and He is the God of love and truth. I do not hate an Englishman. I have spoken much against his institutions, especially the one he has set up in India. But you must not mistake my condemnation of the system for that of the man. My religion requires me to love him as I love myself. I have no interest in living except to prove the faith in me. I would deny God if I do not attempt to prove it at this critical moment."

It must be remembered that all this was at a time when Mr. Gandhi held undisputed sway over the hearts of his three hundred million countrymen. Setting aside all precedence his countrymen unanimously elected Gandhi dictator of the Indian National Congress with full power to lead the country in emergencies. A word from him was sufficient to induce the millions of India to sacrifice their lives without regret or reproach. No man ever commanded the allegiance of so great a number of men, and felt at the same time so meek.

Through the successive stages of "self-denial" and "self-purification" he is gradually preparing his countrymen for the final step in his program, the civil disobedience. Once the country has reached that state, if his program is carried through, the revolution will have been accomplished without shedding a drop of blood. Henry David Thoreau once wrote: "When the officer has resigned office, and the subject has refused allegiance, the revolution is accomplished." That will be the dawn of day, hopeful and bright. The forces of darkness and of evil will have made room for those of light and of love. But this will not come to pass unless Gandhi's policy is literally adopted, and ultimately triumphs. He explains:

> "The political non-violence of the Non-coöperators does not stand the test in the vast majority of cases. Hence the prolongation of the struggle. Let no one blame the unbending English nature. The hardest fiber must melt before the fire of Love. When the British or other nature does not respond, the fire is not strong enough.
>
> "If non-violence is to remain the policy of the nation, we are bound to carry it out to the letter and in the spirit. We must then quickly make up with the English and the Coöperators. We must get their certificate that they feel absolutely safe in our midst, that they regard us as friends, although we belong to a radically different school of thought and politics. We must welcome them to our political platform as honored guests; we must receive them on neutral platforms as comrades. Our non-violence must not breed violence, hatred, or ill-will.
>
> "If we approach our program with the mental reservation that, after all, we shall wrest power from the British by force of arms, then we are untrue to our profession of non-violence.... If we believe in our program, we are bound to believe that the British people are not unamenable to the force of affection, as they undoubtedly are amenable to the force of arms.
>
> "Swaraj is a condition of mind, and the mental condition of India has been challenged.... India will win independence and Swaraj only when the people have acquired strength to die of their own free will. Then there will be Swaraj."

Gandhi has been bitterly assailed by both friends and foes for having consented to render assistance to the cause of the World War in contradiction to his own teachings of non-resistance. Gandhi has been accused of inconsistency and even his most ardent admirers often fail to reconcile his doings during the war with the doctrine of "Ahimsa" (non-violence to any form of life). In his autobiography he has tried to answer these objections, which we shall now examine. He writes:

> "I make no distinction, from the point of view of *ahimsa*, between combatants and non-combatants. He who volunteers to serve a band of dacoits, by working as their carrier, or their watchman while they are about their business, or their nurse when they are wounded, is as much guilty of dacoity as the dacoits themselves. In the same way those who confine themselves to attending to the wounded in battle cannot be absolved from the guilt of war."

This statement shows that his reasons for going into the war were different from those of the Quakers, who think it is an act of Christian love to succor the wounded in war. Gandhi, on the contrary, believes that the person who made bandages for the Red Cross was as much guilty of the murder in war as were the fighting combatants. So long as you have consented to become a part of the machinery of war, whose object is destruction, you are yourself an instrument of destruction. And however you may argue the issue you cannot be absolved from the moral guilt involved. The man who has offered his services as an ambulance carrier on the battlefield is helping the war-lords just as much as his brother who carries arms. One is assisting the cause of the war-lord by killing the enemy, the other by helping war to do its work of murder more efficiently.

I am reminded of the argument I once had with a very conscientious friend of mine, who is a stubborn enemy of war and yet who recalls the following incident in his life with a sorrowful look in his face. One day while he was living in London, a young friend of his came to say his farewell before leaving for the front. Poison gas had been just introduced into the war as a weapon. The combatants were instructed to procure gas masks before departing, but the supply was limited, and his young soldier friend had to go without a gas mask. He left his permit, however, with the request that my friend should get the mask when the next supply came in and send it to his regimental address. Two days later the gas mask was mailed to this boy soldier at the battle front. Before it reached there, however, the soldier was already dead. On the first day after the arrival of the regiment, it was heavily gassed by the enemy, and all of those who had gone without the protective masks were killed. The parcel was returned to my friend at his London address with the sad news that his friend was here no more. He was bitterly disappointed that the mask had not reached the beloved young man in time to save his life. I interpret the whole affair in this way: In sending a gas mask to this English soldier, my pacifist friend was conspiring, however unconsciously, to kill the Germans. He wanted to save his friend from death, but did he realize that at the same time he was wishing more deaths on the enemy? He was, in fact, helping to save one young man in order that this young man might kill more young men on the other side. How does Gandhi justify his action in joining the war, then? We shall let him speak once again. He writes:

> "When two nations are fighting, the duty of a votary of *ahimsa* is to stop the war. He who is not equal to that duty, he who has no power of resisting war, he who is not qualified to resist war, may

> take part in war, and yet whole-heartedly try to free himself, his nation, and the world from war.
>
> "I had hoped to improve my status and that of my people through the British Empire. Whilst in England, I was enjoying the protection of the British fleet, and taking as I did shelter under its armed might, I was directly participating in its potential violence. Therefore if I desired to retain my connection with the Empire and to live under its banner, one of three courses was open to me: I could declare open resistance against the war, and in accordance with the law of Satyagraha, boycott the Empire until it changed its military policy, or I could seek imprisonment by civil disobedience of such of its laws as were fit to be disobeyed, or I could participate in the war on the side of the Empire and thereby acquire the capacity and fitness for resisting the violence of war. I lacked this capacity and fitness, so I thought there was nothing for it but for me to serve in the war."

How far Mr. Gandhi's explanation can answer the objections of his critics we shall leave our readers to judge for themselves. The question is debatable, and admits of differences of opinion. If his argument does not carry conviction with other believers in the doctrine of non-resistance, Gandhi will not be surprised or offended. What an eminent pacifist friend of mine wrote me after she had read the answer of Gandhi may be summed up thus:

Gandhi's argument is entirely wrong. When she was asked to help the Red Cross, she was also told that she had the protection of the army and the navy. To this she replied that she did not wish the protection of the army and the navy. As a conscientious objector to war, she felt it her duty to resist war to the best of her ability and power. When she stood against war with her full might, instead of being a mere cog in the wheel of war, she was like a loose bolt in the machinery. Thus in her resistance "she was a positive force against war."

Such in brief is the man Gandhi. As a specimen of the praise and affection that have been heaped upon him from all quarters, we shall in conclusion give the sketch of Gandhi from the artistic pen of his honest admirer, Mr. Romain Rolland:

> "Soft dark eyes, a small frail man, with a thin face and rather large protruding eyes, his head covered with a little white cap, his body clothed in coarse white cloth, barefooted. He lives on rice and fruit and drinks only water. He sleeps on the floor—sleeps very little, and works incessantly. His body does not seem to count at all. His expression proclaims 'infinite patience and infinite love'. W. W. Pearson, who met him in South Africa, instinctively thought of St. Francis of Assisi. There is an almost childlike simplicity about him. His manner is gentle and courteous even when dealing with adversaries, and he is of immaculate sincerity. He is modest and unassuming, to the point of sometimes seeming almost timid, hesitant, in making an assertion. Yet you feel his

indomitable spirit. Nor is he afraid to admit having been in the wrong. Diplomacy is unknown to him, he shuns oratorical effect or, rather, never thinks about it, and he shrinks unconsciously from the great popular demonstrations organized in his honor. Literally 'ill with the multitude that adores him' he distrusts majorities and fears 'mobocracy' and the unbridled passions of the populace. He feels at ease only in a minority, and is happiest when, in meditative solitude, he listens to the 'still small voice within'."

CHAPTER VI

INDIA'S EXPERIMENT WITH PASSIVE RESISTANCE

In a previous chapter we discussed the character and spirit of Mahatma Gandhi into whose hands has fallen the duty of leading a country of 300 million people through a political revolution. It must be understood, however, that Gandhi is the leader of the revolution and not its creator. Modern thinkers universally admit that individuals or small groups of reformers do not make revolutions. "Agitators or men of genius and ability in a backward community might stir up sporadic revolts and cause minor disturbances, but no human agency can ever create mass revolutions. A successful revolution requires a state of political and social evolution ready for the desired transformation. The history of the world's important political and social revolutions furnishes sufficient evidence in support of this theory."[36] The insurrection of the slaves headed by the able Spartacus, in spite of their early admirable victories, could not overthrow Roman domination. The early attempts of the proletarian revolutionists, supported as they were by leaders of genius and daring, were doomed to failure. India's revolt against English rule in 1857 was ably led, yet it could not succeed. In all these cases the same argument holds. The time was not ripe for the desired change. In the present case, Gandhi has been eminently successful because India was prepared beforehand for a mass revolution. Passive resistance, or no passive resistance, the Indian revolution was bound to come as a necessary consequence of the country's long continued political oppression and economic exploitation. The people were already growing desperate when a united mass uprising was precipitated by the English government's brutal actions of 1919. During the war the English parliament had promised a measure of self-government to the people of India as a reward for their loyalty to the Empire. Early in 1919, when the country was agitating for the promised self-government, the English government of India forcibly passed against the unanimous opposition from all sections of the people, special repressive measures in order to check the spread of nationalism in India. Peaceful demonstrations directed against the newly passed bills were organized all over the country. Once again the government acted harshly in using inhuman methods in the form of public flogging, crawlings and so forth, in the effort to suppress the rising spirit of freedom throughout the land. Just at this time Gandhi came on the stage, and proposed to his countrymen the use of passive resistance for the accomplishment of their political revolution. His resolution of non-violent non-coöperation was

[36] Hyndman.

officially adopted by the Indian National Congress, and the nation in its fight for freedom pledged itself to non-violence. What are passive resistance and non-violent non-coöperation?

"The ethics of passive resistance is very simple and must be known to every student of the New Testament. Passive resistance in its essence is submission to physical force *under protest*. Passive resistance is really a misnomer. No thought is farther away from the heart of the passive resister than the thought of passivity. The soul of his ideal is resistance, and he resists in the most heroic and forceful manner." The only difference between his heroism and our common conception of the word is in the choice of the weapon. His main doctrine is to avoid violence and to substitute for physical force the forces of love, faith, and sacrifice. "Passive resistance resists, but not blow for blow. Passive resistance calls the use of the physical weapon in the hands of man the most cowardly thing in life." Passive resistance teaches men to resist heroically the might and injustice of the untrue and unrighteous. But they must fight with moral and spiritual weapons. They must resist tyranny with forbearance, hatred with love, wrong with right, and injustice with faith. "To hurl back the cowardly weapon of the wicked and the unjust is useless. Let it fall. Bear your suffering with patience. Place your faith in the strength of the divine soul of man." "The hardest fibre must melt before the fire of love. When the results do not correspond, the fire is not strong enough." "The indomitable tenacity and magic of the great soul will operate and win out; force must bow down before heroic gentleness." This is the technique of passive resistance.

The actual application of this principle to politics requires explanation. Individuals or groups have a right to refuse submission to the authority of government which they consider unjust and brutal. "The people of India," says Gandhi, "have been convinced, after long and fearful trials, that the English government of India is Satanic. It is based on violence. Its object is not the good of the people, but rapine and plunder. It works not in the interests of the governed, and its policies are not guided by their consent. It bases itself finally not on right but on might. Its last appeal is not to the reason, nor the heart, but to the sword. The country is tired of this creed and it has risen against it." Under these conditions the most straightforward course to follow is to seek the destruction of such an institution. The people of India can destroy the thing by force, or else they can refuse their coöperation with its various activities and render it helpless; then refuse their submission to its authority and render it useless.

Just consider the case of a country where all government officers resign from their offices, where the people boycott the various governmental institutions such as public schools and colleges, law courts, and legislatures; and where the taxpayers refuse to pay their taxes. The people can do all this without resort to force, and so stop the machinery of the government dead, and make it a meaningless thing without use and power. To quote Thoreau once again: "When the officer has resigned office, and the subject has refused allegiance, the revolution is accomplished." This is exactly what the people of India have set out to do by their present policy of passive resistance. However simple the theory may be, the practice of it is difficult and perilous. When a people resort to these peaceful means for the accomplishment of political revolution, they must be prepared to undergo unlimited suffering. The enemy's camp will be determined and organized; from it will issue constant provocations and brutal exhibitions of force. Under these difficult circumstances, the only chance for the success of the passive resister is in his readiness for infinite and courageous suffering, qualities that in turn imply a powerful reserve of self-control and an utter dedication to the ideal. Evidently to prepare a nation of 300 million people for this tremendous task must take time and require great patience and courage. To quote Gandhi:

> "Non-coöperation is not a movement of brag, bluster, or bluff. It is a test of our sincerity. It requires solid and silent self-sacrifice. It challenges our honesty and our capacity for national work. It is a movement that aims at translating ideas into action."

The people of India are moving on the road to freedom with dignity. They are slowly nearing their goal. On their way the passive resisters are learning their lessons from bitter experience, and are growing stronger in faith every day. That they are headed in the right direction and are quietly pushing forward we do know in a definite way, but when they will emerge victorious we cannot say. To help the reader to catch the subtle spirit behind this movement, we shall quote a few more lines from the pen of its leader:

> "I am a man of peace. I believe in peace. But I do not want peace at any price. I do not want the peace that you find in stone. I do not want the peace that you find in the grave; but I do want peace which you find embedded in the human breast, which is exposed to the arrows of the whole world, but which is protected from all harm by the power of the Almighty God."

The wearing of home-spun cloth by all classes of people, rich and poor alike, is one of the most important items in the non-coöperative program. Yet every time I have tried to justify it before my American friends, I have received as response a shrug of the shoulders. Not only the layman, but serious students of economics have replied: "That is going back into mediæval ways. In these days of machinery home-spinning is sheer foolishness." Yet one does not have to be an economist to know that "labor spent on home-spinning and thus used in the creation of a utility, is better spent than wasted in idleness." The majority of the population of India lives directly upon the produce of the soil. They remain in forced idleness for a greater part of the year. There are no industries in the country, cottage or urban. So the people have nothing to occupy them during their idle months. Before the English conquest, agricultural India had its supplementary industries on which the people could fall during their idle time. But these industries have been completely destroyed by the English fiscal policy for India, which was formulated with the desire to build England's own fabric and other industries upon the ruins of India's industries. The country produces more cotton than is needed for its own use. Under ordinary conditions this cotton is exported out of the country, and cloth manufactured in the mills of England is imported into the country for its consumption. For want of a substitute people are forced to buy this foreign cloth. And they are so miserably poor that the great majority of them cannot afford one meal a day. Nothing could be more sensible for these people than to adopt home-spinning during their idle hours. This will help to save them, partially at least, from starvation. Let me quote Gandhi on this subject:

> "I claim for the spinning-wheel the properties of a musical instrument, for whilst a hungry and a naked woman will refuse to dance to the accompaniment of a piano, I have seen women beaming with joy to see the spinning-wheel work, for they know that they can through that rustic instrument both feed and clothe themselves.
>
> "Yes, it does solve the problem of India's chronic poverty and is an insurance against famine....
>
> "When spinning was almost compulsorily stopped nothing replaced it except slavery and idleness. Our mills cannot today spin enough for our wants, and if they did, they will not keep down prices unless they were compelled. They are frankly money-makers and will not therefore regulate prices according to the needs of the nation. Hand-spinning is therefore designed to put millions of rupees in the hands of poor villagers. Every agricultural country requires a supplementary industry to enable the peasants to utilise the spare hours. Such industry for India has always been spinning. Is it such a visionary ideal—an attempt to revive an ancient occupation whose destruction has brought on slavery, pauperism and disappearance of the inimitable artistic talent which was once all expressed in the wonderful fabric of India and which was the envy of the world?"

The people of India have made mistakes in the past, and they will probably make others in the future. But that in sticking to non-violence they are fulfilling the noblest ideal ever conceived by man, and in staying loyal to the spirit of passive resistance they are following a truer and a richer light will not be questioned. Will humanity at large see the wisdom of passive resistance? To me in our present state that seems very doubtful. It will be easy to convince the common man of the virtue and wisdom of non-violence. But unfortunately the reins of our destiny are not in the hands of common people. Those who hold the power over the nations of the world have other interests to look after than the common interests of the average man. They are pledged to the service of other masters whose welfare is not the welfare of the whole race. "The world is ruled at the present day by those who must oppress and kill in order to exploit." So long as this condition continues, there is little hope for the reformation of human society. We must all suffer because we would not learn.

Mankind will not always refuse to listen to the voice of reason. A time will come when the great masses all over the world will refuse to fight, when exploitation and wars will cease, and the different groups of the human race will consent to live together in coöperation and peace.

An illustration of the might of passive resistance was furnished during the conflict between the British Government of India and the Akali Sikhs over the management of their shrines. This incident shows to what heights of self-sacrifice and suffering human beings can reach when they are under the spell of noble idealism. Sikhs are a virile race of fighting people. They are all members of a religious fellowship and form nearly one-sixth of the population of the province of Punjab in the northwest part of India. They constitute by themselves a very important community, which is closely bound together by a feeling of common brotherhood. They all go by the name of Singh, meaning the lion, and are rightly proud of their history, which though brief in scope of time, is yet full of inspiring deeds committed by the Sikh forefathers in the defense of religious freedom and justice during the evil days of a few corrupt and fanatic Moghul rulers of India. As a rule Sikhs belong to the agriculturist class and both men and women are stalwart and healthy-looking. Their men are distinguished by their long hair and beards. They are born with martial characteristics and are naturally very bold and brave in their habits. Once aroused to sense of duty towards the weak and the oppressed, they have always been found willing to give their lives without remorse or regret. Sikhs constitute a major portion of the military and police forces of India and of several British colonies. Those tourists who have been in the East will recall the tall, bearded Sikh policemen of the British principalities of Shanghai and Hongkong. Since the Sepoy Mutiny of 1857, Sikhs have always been regarded as the most loyal and devoted subjects of the British Crown in India. "On the battlefields of Flanders, Mesopotamia, Persia, and Egypt they have served the Empire faithfully and well. Their deeds of heroism were particularly noticed during the most trying moments of the World War."

Before the British acquired the province in 1849 Sikhs were the rulers of the Punjab. During the period of their rule Sikh princes had made rich grants of land and other property to the historic temples and shrines of their religion. Because of the introduction of irrigation canals some of these properties have acquired immense values in recent years, their annual incomes in several cases running up to a million rupees or more.

The Sikhs have always regarded the temple properties as belonging to the community. And when it was brought to the notice of their progressive leaders that the hereditary priests at some of the historic and rich Sikh centers had become corrupt and were wasting the temple money in vicious pleasures, the Sikhs organized the Central Shrine Management Committee. The object of the committee was to take away the management of all important Sikh shrines from the corrupt priests and to vest it in the community. The committee was first organized in November, 1920, and its members were elected on the basis of universal franchise open to both sexes. The method of procedure followed by the committee was that of arbitration. A local sub-committee, consisting of the leading Sikhs in the neighborhood, was formed to watch over the affairs of every shrine. This sub-committee was to act in coöperation with the temple priest, who was henceforth to be a subordinate and not the sole master. Whenever the priests agreed to arbitrate the matter in a fair manner, they were allowed free use of their residence quarters and were awarded liberal salaries for household expenses. By this method the Central

Shrine Committee in a short time became masters of some of the very rich and important Sikh shrines.

While in several of the smaller places such transfer of ownership was accomplished through peaceful means, in some of the bigger temples the community had to undergo heavy losses in life. For instance at Nanakana Sahib, the Jerusalem of the Sikhs, a band of one hundred unarmed followers of the Central Committee were surrounded by a band of armed hirelings of the priest. They were first shot at, then assaulted with rifle butt-ends, and later cut into small pieces or burnt alive after being previously soaked with kerosene oil. The priest personally supervised this whole affair of daylight butchery which did not finish until the last one of the Sikhs had been consumed by the bloody bonfire. Later it was discovered that the priest had prepared for the bloodshed long before, and that he had hired the armed ruffians and barricaded the temple premises after consultation with the local English Justice of the Peace. The leading dailies of the country openly stated that the English civil commissioner was a co-partner in the crime, but the government took no notice of the fact. The Hindu population was not surprised that the priest who had murdered one hundred innocent, inoffensive, devout Sikhs escaped capital punishment in the British courts or that in his prison he was surrounded with all the princely luxuries of his former palace.

Guru Ka Bagh is a historic Sikh temple, situated at a distance of nearly eight miles from the central headquarters of the Sikhs in the city of Amritsar. Through an agreement drawn between the Central Shrine Committee and the temple priest on January 31, 1921, Guru Ka Bagh had come under the management of a local board assisted by the priest. Six months later, presumably at the suggestion of the civil commissioner, the priest burned all the temple records and drove the representative of the Central Committee out of the temple premises; whereupon the Central Committee took full charge of the temple. They were in uncontested possession of the premises until trouble started, a year later, from the arrest of five Akali Sikhs, who had gone out to cut firewood from the surrounding grounds attached to the Guru Ka Bagh. A formal complaint was obtained by the civil commissioner from the ousted priest to the effect that in cutting wood for use in the temple kitchen the Akalis were trespassing on his property rights. The cutting of wood on the premises went on as usual until the police began to make wholesale arrests of all so-called trespassers.

This procedure continued for four days till the police found out that large numbers of Akalis (immortals) were pouring in from all sides, everyone eager to be arrested in protecting the rights of his community. Then the police began to beat the Akali bands with bamboo sticks six feet long and fitted with iron knobs on both ends. As soon as Akalis, in groups of five, started to go across for cutting wood, they were assaulted by the police armed with these bamboo sticks and were mercilessly beaten over their heads and bodies until they became unconscious and had to be carried away by the temple ambulance workers.

The news of this novel method of punishment at once spread throughout the country like wild fire and thousands of Sikhs started on their way to Amritsar. The government closed the sale of railroad tickets to all Akali Sikhs wearing black turbans, which constituted their national uniform. The various highways leading into the city of the Golden Temple, Amritsar, were blocked by armed police. But after a call for them had been issued at the official headquarters of the Central Shrine Management Committee, nothing could stop the Akalis from crowding into the city. Where railroads refused passage they walked long distances on foot, and when river and canal bridges were guarded against them, both men and women swam across the waters to reach their holy temple at Amritsar. In the course of two days the huge premises of the Golden Temple were filled with Akalis of every sort and kind—boys of twelve with feet sore with blisters from prolonged walking, women of all ages—and still many were fast pouring in.

"Among them were medaled veterans of many wars who had fought for the English in foreign lands and won eminent recognition, and had now rushed to Amritsar to win a higher and nobler merit in the service of their religion and country. They had assembled there to be ruthlessly beaten and killed by the agents of the same government for whose protection they had fought at home and across the seas." These old warriors, disillusioned by their English friends, who were now conspiring to take from them the simple rights of worship in their own temples, had not lost their independence and courage. They had always been the first to leap before the firing guns of the enemy on the battlefields of England; they were first again here to throw themselves at the feet of their Central Shrine Committee, willing to sacrifice their lives at its bidding. All were eager, one more than the other, to offer themselves for the beating at Guru Ka Bagh.

Seeing that their efforts to stop the Akalis from gathering at Amritsar had been wholly unsuccessful, the Government issued strict orders against any person or group of persons from proceeding to Guru Ka Bagh. Sizing up the whole situation, the assembled leaders of the community represented in the Central Shrine Committee at once resolved on two things. First, the community would contest its right of peaceful pilgrimage and worship at Guru Ka Bagh and other temples until the last among the Sikhs had been killed in the struggle. Secondly, they would steadfastly adhere to the letter and spirit of Mahatma Gandhi's teachings of non-violence. Thirdly, they decided to send Akalis to Guru Ka Bagh in batches of a hundred each, in direct defiance of the orders of the British Government. Before starting on the march, each Akali was required to take an oath of strict non-violence; that he would not use force in action or speech under any provocation whatsoever; that if assaulted he would submit to the rough treatment with resignation and humility; that whatever might be the nature of his ordeal he would not turn his face backward. He would either reach Guru Ka Bagh and go out for chopping wood when so instructed, or he would be carried to the committee's emergency hospital unconscious, dead or alive.

The first batch started towards Guru Ka Bagh on August 31, 1922, after previously taking the vow of non violence. The Akalis were dressed in black turbans with garlands of white flowers wrapped around their heads. On their way, as the Akalis sang their religious hymns in chorus, they were met by a band of policemen armed with bamboo sticks. Simultaneously the Akalis sat down and thrust their heads forward to receive blows. An order was given by the English superintendent, and on rushed the police with their long bamboo rods to do their bloody work. They beat the non-resisting Sikhs on the heads, backs, and other delicate parts of their bodies, until the entire one hundred was maimed and battered and lay there in a mass unconscious, prostrate, bleeding. While the volunteers were passively receiving blows from the police, the English superintendent sportively ran his horse over them and back. His assistants pulled the Sikhs by their sacred hair, spat upon their faces, and cursed and called them names in the most offensive manner. Later, their unconscious bodies were dragged away by the long hair and thrown into the mud on either side of the road. From the ditches they were picked up by the ambulance workers and brought to the emergency hospital under the management of the Central Shrine Committee.

In this way batches of one hundred, pledged to the principle of non-violence, were sent every day to be beaten by the police in this brutal fashion and then were picked up unconscious by the ambulance service. After the tenth day Akalis were allowed to proceed freely on their way. But the beatings in Guru Ka Bagh at the stop where wood for kitchen use had been cut, continued till much later. After a few over fifteen hundred non-resistant and innocent human beings had been thus sacrificed, several hundred of whom had died of injuries received and many others had been totally disabled for life, the Government withdrew the police from Guru Ka Bagh and allowed the Sikhs free use of the temple and its adjoining properties.

It was an acknowledgment of defeat on the part of the British Government and a definite victory for the passive resisters. Non-violence had triumphed over brute force. The meek Sikhs had established their moral and spiritual courage beyond a doubt. Those who earlier had laughed at Gandhi's doctrines now began to reconsider their opinions and wondered if it were not true that the soul force of man was the mightiest power in the world, more powerful than the might of all its armies and navies put together. "Socrates and Christ are both dead, but their spirits live and will continue to live." Their bodies were destroyed by those who possessed physical force, but their souls were invincible. Who could conquer the spirit of Socrates, Christ, or Gandhi when that spirit refused to be conquered? At the time of the Guru Ka Bagh incident the physical Gandhi was locked behind iron bars in a jail of India, but his spirit accompanied every Sikh as he stepped across the line to receive the enemy's cowardly blows.

The amazing part of this whole story is the perfect peace that prevailed throughout its entire course. The program of passive resistance was carried to completion without one slip of action on the part of the passive resisters. No community in the whole length and breadth of India is more warlike and more inflammable for a righteous cause than the Sikhs; and nothing is more provoking to a Sikh than an insult offered to his sacred hair. Yet in hundreds of cases their sacred hair was smeared with mud and trampled upon, while the bodies of non-resisting Sikhs were dragged by their hair in the most malicious manner by the police; but the passive resisters remained firm in their resolve to the last and thereby proved their faith both in themselves and in their principles.

Those who have not grasped the subtle meaning of passive resistance will call the Akali Sikhs cowards. They will say: "Well, the reason why the Akalis did not return the blows of the police was because they were afraid; and it was cowardice and not courage that made them submit to such insults as the pulling of their sacred hair and so forth. A truly brave person, who has a grain of salt in him, will answer the blows of the enemy under those conditions and fight in the defense of his honor until he is killed." Although we do not agree with the first part of our objecting friend's argument, we shall admit the truth of his statement that it takes a brave man to defend his honor at the risk of death itself. Yet we hold that the Akali who, while defending his national rights, voluntarily allowed himself to be beaten to death without thoughts of malice or hatred in his heart against anybody was a more courageous person than even the hero of our objecting friend. Why? To use Gandhi's illustration: "What do you think? Wherein is courage required—in blowing others to pieces from behind a cannon or with a smiling face approaching a cannon and being blown to pieces? Who is the true warrior—he who keeps death as a bosom-friend or he who controls the death of others? Believe me that a man devoid of courage and manhood can never be a passive resister."

Let us stretch the point a little further in order to make it more clear. During the martial law days at Amritsar in 1919, the commanding officer ordered that all persons passing through a certain lane, where previously an Englishwoman had been assaulted by a furious mob, should be made to crawl on the bellies. Those living in the neighborhood had submitted to this humiliation at the point of British bayonets. Later, when Mahatma Gandhi visited the lane, he is reported to have made a speech from the spot which may be summarized thus: "You Punjabees, who possess muscular bodies and have statures six feet tall; you, who call yourselves brave, submitted to the soul-degrading crawling order. I am a small man and my physique is very weak. I weigh less than a hundred pounds. But there is no power in this world that can make *me* crawl on my belly. General Dyer's soldiers can bind my body and put me in jail, or with their military weapons they can take my life; but when he orders me to crawl on my belly I shall say: 'Oh foolish man, don't you see, God has given me two feet to walk on? Why shall I crawl on my knees, then?'" This is an instance of passive resistance. Under these circumstances, would you call Gandhi a coward? You must remember this distinction between a coward and a passive resister: a coward submits to force through fear; while a passive resister submits to force *under protest*. In our illustration of the crawling order those persons who had submitted to the order because they were afraid of the punishment involved if they disobeyed it were cowards of the first degree. But Gandhi would be a passive resister, and you would not call him a coward, would you?

Let me give you a sample of the sublime heroism displayed by the Akalis at Guru Ka Bagh. In one instance the policeman's blow struck an Akali with such violence that one of his eyeballs dropped out. His eye was bleeding profusely, but still he walked forward towards his goal until he was knocked down the second time and fell on the ground unconscious. Another Akali, Pritipal Singh, was knocked down eight times. Each time as soon as he recovered his senses, he stood on his feet and started to go forward, until after the eighth time he lay on the ground wholly prostrate. I have known Pritipal Singh in India. We went to school together for five years. Pritipal was a good boy in every way. He was the strongest person in our school and yet the meekest of all men. He had a very jolly temper, and I can hear to this day his loud ringing laugh. Inoffensive in his habits, he was a cultured and a loving friend. When I read his name in the papers and later discovered how cruelly he suffered from the injuries which finally resulted in his premature death, I was indeed sorrowful. That such a saintly person as Pritipal Singh should be made to go through such hellish tortures and that his life should be thus cruelly ended in the prime of youth was enough to give anyone a shock. But when I persuaded myself that with the passing of that handsome youth there was one more gone for truth's sake, I felt peaceful and happy once more.

Lest the reader be at a loss to know what this whole drama of horrible tortures on the one hand and supernatural courage on the other was all about, we shall give the gist of the whole affair as follows:

At the time when the issue was precipitated in Guru Ka Bagh the Central Shrine Management Committee had already acquired control over many of the rich Sikh shrines, and become a powerful force in the uplift of the community. The committee was receiving huge incomes from the various shrine properties, which it proposed to spend on educational and social service work. Those at the helm of affairs were profoundly nationalistic in their views. Naturally, the British Government began to fear their power, which it desired to break through suppression. Hence the issue at Guru Ka Bagh was not the chopping of fuel wood. The ghastly motive of the Government was to cow the Sikhs and crush their spirits through oppression. How it started to demonstrate its power and how shamefully it failed in its sinister purpose has already been explained.

Many other examples of the victory of soul force over brute strength could be cited from the recent history of India. I chose the Guru Ka Bagh affair as the subject of my illustration for two reasons. In the first place, it was the most simple and yet the most prominent demonstration of the holiness and might of passive resistance; and secondly, the drama was performed in my own home town by actors who belonged to my own community and were kith and kin to me in the sense that I could know fully their joys and sorrows, their hopes and fears.

CHAPTER VII

JALLIANWALLA MASSACRE AT AMRITSAR

In this chapter we shall relate briefly the story of what occurred in Punjab during the troubled days of 1919. These incidents, popularly known as "the Punjab wrongs," led to far-reaching consequences in the relationship between England and India, and knowledge of them is very necessary for a proper understanding of what has happened in India since. We shall begin with the beginning of the World War and follow the various incidents in the sequence of their occurrence.

It is a matter of common knowledge now that the people of India supported the British Empire throughout the period of the war in a very liberal and enthusiastic manner. "India's contributions to the war both in its quota of man-force and money were far beyond the capacity of its poor inhabitants." Leaders of all states of opinion joined hands to assist the Empire in its time of need. It has been stated before that Gandhi overworked in the capacity as an honorary recruiting officer until he contracted dysentery, which at one time threatened to prove fatal.

India was "bled white" in order to win the war. But for her support in men and money England would have suffered greatly in prestige. Except for Indian troops the German advance to Paris in the fall of 1914 might not have been checked. The official publication, "India's Contribution to the Great War," describes the work of the Indian troops thus:

> "The Indian Corps reached France in the nick of time and helped to stem the great German thrust towards Ypres and the Channel Ports during the Autumn of 1914. These were the only trained reinforcements immediately available in any part of the British Empire and right worthily they played their part.
>
> "In Egypt and Palestine, in Mesopotamia, Persia, East and West Africa and in subsidiary theatres they shared with their British and Dominion comrades the attainment of final victory."[37]

While the issue of the war still seemed doubtful, the British Parliament, in order to induce the people of India to still greater efforts in their support of the Empire, held out definite promises of self-government to India after the war as a reward for their loyalty. Mr. Montague, His Majesty's Secretary of State for India, made the following announcement on August 20, 1917:

> "The policy of His Majesty's Government with which the

[37] Page 221. Quoted from Lajpat Rai's *Unhappy India*.

> Government of India are in complete accord, is that of the increasing association of Indians in every branch of the administration and the gradual development of self-governing institutions with a view to the progressive realisation of responsible government in India as an integral part of the British Empire. They have decided that substantial steps in this direction should be taken as soon as possible, ..."

The text of the above announcement was widely published in the entire press of India. Then followed the famous message of President Woodrow Wilson to the Congress with its definite pledge of "self-determination" to subordinate nations. This helped to brighten still more India's hopes for home-rule.

Naturally, after the Armistice was signed, the people of India expected the fulfilment of the war promises. "But the British Government, anticipating that soon after the war ended there would be a loud clamor in the country for home-rule, gave instead of self-government the Rowlatt Act, which was designed to stifle the nationalistic spirit in its infancy." The act gave unlimited power to the police to prohibit public assemblies, to order indiscriminate searches of private homes, to make arrests without notification, and so forth. "Its main purpose was in such a manner to strengthen the authority of the police and to enable them to root out of the country every form of liberal and independent thought." The plans of the British Bureaucracy were, however, defeated in their entirety, because the passage of the act did not go through the Legislative Assembly as smoothly as was expected. The whole country cried out in one voice against the Rowlatt Act, but it was passed by the British Government of India in the teeth of the *unanimous* opposition of *all* elected as well as government appointed Indian members of the Legislative Council.

This was once again followed by mass meetings and parades in protest, petitions to the British Parliament, delegations to the Viceroy, and a nation-wide demonstration against the Rowlatt Act. But the Government altogether ignored the sentiments of the country in this matter, an attitude which in turn helped to inflame the masses still more.

Gandhi considered the existence of the act on the statute books of India a national humiliation, and in protest he ordered the people of India to observe April 6, 1919, as a day of fast and national *hartal*. *Hartal* is the sign of deep mourning, during which the whole business of the country is stopped and the people wander about the streets in grief and lamentation. It was observed in ancient times only at the death of popular kings or on the occasion of some other very serious national calamity.

The response to Gandhi's appeal for the *hartal* was very general. It was surprising how quickly the sentiment of national consciousness had spread throughout the country. Overnight Gandhi's name was on the lips of everybody, and even the most ignorant countrywomen were talking about the Rowlatt Act. I remember that on the afternoon of April the 6th, while I was walking toward the site of the mass meeting in my town, the like of which were being held all over India, and at which resolutions of protest against the Rowlatt Act were passed, I saw a girl of six nearly collapse on the street. After I had picked her up, and she had rested from the heat of the sun, I asked her who she was and where she was going. The little girl replied: "I am the daughter of *Bharat Mata* (Mother India) and I am going to the funeral of Daulat (Rowlatt). Mahatma Dandhi (Gandhi) has called me."

The day passed quite peacefully except for slight disturbances in a few places. But the excitement throughout the country, particularly in the Punjab, was very great. The situation was so tense that Gandhi sent his strong admonitions of non-violence to his people in a continual stream. The activity at Amritsar started when, on the morning of April 10th the English Commissioner invited Dr. Kitchlew and Dr. Satyapal, the two popular young leaders of the city, to his residence and ordered their deportation to some unknown place. When it became known that their leaders had been treacherously removed the citizens went on a sudden *hartal*, and a huge mob began to gather in front of the main city gate. The mob soon organized itself into a procession, which started to move toward the District Commissioner's residence to request the restoration of Doctors Kitchlew and Satyapal. While crossing the railroad bridge, the procession was met by armed police who soon caused six casualties among the peaceful, unarmed mob. The mob soon turned back and fell upon the city in a wild fury. It divided itself into different groups and expended its rage by setting fire to the city hall, two English banks, and a local Christian church. Two bank managers, the only Englishmen present in town on that day, were cruelly murdered. An English nurse who happened to be passing through a narrow street was also assaulted by the mob, but was soon rescued by the citizens and carried to a place of safety. Later on, this benevolent Christian lady greatly endeared herself to the people of Amritsar by refusing to accept any other indemnity for the assault than the price of her wrist watch which was lost in the scramble.

Immediately after the news of Amritsar reached the other towns in the province, similar outbreaks of popular frenzy occurred in many places, with this difference however, that at no other place besides Amritsar were English residents injured. There were casualties on the side of the mob everywhere, but none on the side of the English. On April 11th the authority of the civil government was withdrawn, and martial law was declared in most sections of the province of Punjab.

Thus did the trouble begin that resulted in the massacre of Amritsar. On that fatal day, April 13th, a mass meeting had been announced to take place in Jallianwalla Bagh, an open enclosure in the heart of the city of Amritsar. As it happened, April 13th was also the Baisakhi day, which is observed all over India as a day of national festival. Large crowds of country people had gathered into the city on that account. On the morning of the 13th, General Dyer, the commanding officer of the city, issued from the headquarters an order prohibiting the Jallianwalla Bagh meeting, and notices to that effect were posted in several places in the city. It should be mentioned here that unlike the towns of America, there were in Amritsar at the time no universally read daily papers which could convey the Commanding Officer's order all around in the short interval between its issue and the time of the meeting. Under these circumstances General Dyer's prohibitory order could reach only a small fraction of the people in the city.

Now let us come to the scene of the meeting. People began to assemble in Jallianwalla Bagh at 3 o'clock. There were old men, women who carried babies in their arms, and children who held toys in their hands. They were all dressed in their holiday gala-dresses. "While a few had come there to attend the meeting knowingly, the majority had just followed the crowd and drifted in the Bagh out of simple curiosity." Whatever may have been its nature otherwise, it is certain that the crowd at the Jallianwalla was not composed of bloody revolutionists. Not one of them carried even a walking stick. They had assembled there in the open inclosure peacefully to listen to speeches and perhaps at the end to pass a few resolutions. At four o'clock the meeting was called to order, and the speeches began. No more than forty minutes of this peaceful gathering, and the audience were listening in an attentive and orderly manner to the speaker who stood on a raised platform in the center, when General Dyer walked in with his band of thirty soldiers and suddenly opened fire on the crowd without giving them any warning or chance to disperse. There was a sudden wild skirmish in the inclosure. People began to run toward all sides to save their lives; those who fell down were run over by the rest and crushed under their weight. Others who attempted to escape by leaping over the low wall on the east end were shot dead by the fire from the general's squad. As the crowd centered near the only escape from the unfinished low wall, the general directed his shots there. He aimed where the crowd was the thickest, and inside of the fifteen minutes during which his ammunition lasted he had killed at least eight hundred men, women, and children and wounded many times that number.

It was already late afternoon when General Dyer, his ammunition having run out, departed to his headquarters without providing any kind of succor or medical aid to the wounded who lay bleeding and helpless at the scene of slaughter. Before the people of the neighborhood recovered from their consternation, it had already begun to get dark. As one of the rules of martial law strictly forbade walking in the streets of Amritsar after dark, it was impossible for any person or group of persons to bring organized relief to the wounded at Jallianwalla. The horrible agonies of those that lay in the Bagh disabled and deserted were heard with grim patience all through the night by the faithful wife Rattan Devi, when she sat there "in the midst of that ghastly human carnival" holding in her lap the dead body of her beloved husband. She had run to the scene after the shooting in a mad search for her husband. After she had looked underneath a dozen heaps of dead bodies and stumbled over many others, her eyes were drawn to the spot where her husband's dead body lay flat on the ground. Rattan Devi's husband was already dead and beyond human aid. The devoted wife could not restore the dead man to life, but how could she afford to leave his lifeless body in the stark neighborhood over night? She was too weak to carry it home all by herself and there was no aid available. So she sat there through the night holding a dead man in her lap.

The horrors of that night of suffering were related by Rattan Devi in her evidence before the Indian National Congress sub-committee, in which she described "the fearful agony of dying human beings, who kept crying for drinks of water all through the night." No friendly aid came to these departing souls in their last hours of deep distress. Afraid of General Dyer's deadly vengeance their fellowmen had stayed away, while dogs from the neighboring streets wandered freely inside the Bagh to feast on the bleeding human bodies.

At the following session of the Indian National Congress which was held at Amritsar, I myself saw at its exhibition twenty pairs of little shoes, belonging to babies from a few months to a year old. These had been picked up in the Jallianwalla Bagh by various persons after the shooting, and they belonged to twenty innocent babies in their mothers' laps who had been completely obliterated in the mad scramble that had accompanied the shooting. All that was left of these children was those tiny shoes. May God bless the souls of the dear little ones and many others who fell victims to the haughty general's bloody mood on the thirteenth of April, 1919, at Jallianwalla Bagh.

Later, when General Dyer was cross-examined before Lord Hunter's Committee, which was appointed by the British Parliament to report on Punjab disturbances, he testified to the following:

1. That there was no provocation on the part of the people of Amritsar for the Jallianwalla Bagh massacre either on the day of the shooting or immediately before it. He had the situation well in hand and the atmosphere was quite calm and peaceful.

2. That his order prohibiting the meeting was issued the morning before the meeting and reached only a fraction of the people in Amritsar on that festival day of the thirteenth.

3. That when he arrived on the scene of the meeting with his squad, he found the people listening to the speaker in a calm manner and there was no show of resistance offered to him. On the other hand, on seeing him enter the premises, the audience began to run off in all directions.

4. That he opened fire at the assembled meeting without giving the people any warning or chance to disperse, and he continued firing while his ammunition lasted—all the time directing his shots at places where the crowd was the thickest.

5. That he had brought a machine gun with him, which he had to leave outside because the lane was too narrow for it to enter. And he admitted that the casualties would have been much greater if he had been able to use the machine gun.

6. That his reason for the massacre at the Jallianwalla was to teach the people a lesson, and he did not stop shooting after the crowd had begun to disperse because he was afraid they would laugh at him. The general wanted to show the people the might of the British rule.

7. That he did not think to or care to provide succor to the wounded at Jallianwalla. It was not a part of his business.

Reproduced below is a part of General Dyer's testimony before Lord Hunter's committee:

"Q. When you got into the Bagh what did you do? A. I opened fire.

Q. At once? A. Immediately. I had thought about the matter and don't imagine it took me more than thirty seconds to make up my mind as to what my duty was.

Q. How many people were in the crowd? A. I then estimated them roughly at 5,000. I heard afterwards there were many more.

Q. On the assumption that there was that risk of people being in the crowd who were not aware of the proclamation, did it not occur to you that it was a proper measure to ask the crowd to disperse before you took that step of actually firing? A. No, at the time I did not. I merely felt that my orders had not been obeyed, that martial law was flouted, and that it was my duty to immediately disperse by rifle fire.

Q. When you left Rambagh [his headquarters] did it occur to you that you might have to fire? A. Yes, I had considered the nature of the duty that I might have to face.

Q. Did the crowd at once start to disperse as soon as you fired? A. Immediately.

Q. Did you continue firing? A. Yes.

Q. What reason had you to suppose that if you had ordered the assembly to leave the Bagh, they would not have done so without the necessity of your firing and continuing firing for any length of time? A. Yes, I think it quite possible that I could have dispersed them perhaps even without firing.

Q. Why did you not have recourse to that? A. They would have all come back and laughed at me, and I should have made what I considered a fool of myself.

Q. And on counting the ammunition it was found that 1,650 rounds of ammunition had been fired? A. Quite right.

Q. Supposing the passage was sufficient to allow the armoured cars to go in, would you have opened fire with the machine guns? A. I think, probably, yes.

Q. In that case the casualties would have been very much higher? A. Yes.

Q. I take it that your idea in taking that action was to strike terror? A. Call it what you like. I was going to punish them. My idea from the military point of view was to make a wide impression."

During the course of its history mankind has witnessed many massacres of a bloody and ruthless nature, but in every case before a massacre occurred, there was a provocation of some kind. Jallianwalla Bagh stands out unique in this respect—that it was an unprovoked, premeditated and pre-arranged, coldblooded massacre of at least eight hundred innocent men, women, and children, who were assembled in a peaceful meeting on the day of their national festival, with no thought of evil in their minds nor any desire to offer resistance of any sort or kind to anybody.

The most interesting part of the story is that what had happened at Jallianwalla Bagh on the thirteenth of April was considered so trivial and unimportant a matter that it took four months for the news to reach official London. After the report of Lord Hunter's committee had been published, and all the horrible details of the massacre were fully disclosed, General Dyer was retired from the military service on full pension. But on his return to England he was handed a purse of ten thousand pounds sterling, which amount had been raised by voluntary subscription by the English people to recompense the general for his heroic work at Jallianwalla Bagh. Such was the reaction of the English nation to the massacre.

Gandhi's interpretation of General Dyer's "heroism" is, however, different. He writes:

> "He [General Dyer] has called an unarmed crowd of men and children—mostly holiday-makers—'a rebel army.' He believes himself to be the saviour of Punjab in that he was able to shoot down like rabbits men who were penned in an enclosure. Such a man is unworthy of being considered a soldier. There was no bravery in his action. He ran no risk. He shot without the slightest opposition and without warning. This is not an 'error of judgment'. It is a paralysis of it in the face of fancied danger. It is proof of criminal incapacity and heartlessness."

The reader will be in a position now to understand the meaning of Mahatma Gandhi's letter to the Viceroy of India, dated August 1, 1920, and quoted on page 56 in which Gandhi gave his reasons for his decision not to coöperate with the British Government of India. It may be recalled that one of Mahatma Gandhi's reasons was the "callous disregard of the feelings of Indians" betrayed by the House of Lords. It must be remembered here also that the massacre of Jallianwalla occurred on April 13, 1919, and it was exactly a year and three months later that Mahatma Gandhi made his decision to boycott the British Government. During this interval he had persistently hoped for a change in the British attitude.

The massacre at Jallianwalla was only one part of the awful Punjab story. What occurred at Amritsar and other towns in the province during the martial days of 1919 was even more shameful and unworthy, "on account of the outrage of human dignity it involved." The issuing of crawling orders and the throwing of bombs from aeroplanes over peaceful towns constituted in part the doings of the military and police during the unfortunate days of martial law. Nor was that all. Mrs. Sarojini Naidu, the first woman president of India, said while speaking on the "Punjab wrongs" before a large London audience (Kingsway Hall, June 3, 1919):

> "My sisters were flogged, they were stripped naked; they were outraged."

The ingenuity of the English officials during the martial law period in inventing fancy punishments showed itself conspicuously in the town of Kasur where, according to the findings of the Congress sub-committee,

"1. School boys and men were whipped, 'with no particular object,' and there was no question of any martial law offense. Prostitutes were invited to witness the ceremony.

2. People were made to mark time and climb ladders.

3. Religious mendicants were washed with lime.

4. Those who failed to salute Europeans were made to rub their roses on the ground.

6. Public gallows were erected which were later abandoned. In all, eighteen persons were hanged in the Punjab during the martial law regime, many of whom were totally innocent."

We shall give below the evidence of Gurdevi, the widow of Mangal Jat, before the Congress sub-committee on what had occured at Manianwalla:

> "One day, during the Martial Law period, Mr. Bosworth Smith gathered together all the males of over eight years at the Dacca Dalia Bungalow, which is some miles from our village, in connection with the investigations that were going on. Whilst the men were at the Bungalow, he rode to our village, taking back with him all the women who met him on the way carrying food for their men at the Bungalow. Reaching the village, he went around the lanes and ordered all women to come out of their houses, himself forcing them out with sticks. He made us all stand near the village Daira. The women folded their hands before him. He beat some with his stick and spat at them and used the foulest and most unmentionable language. He hit me twice and spat in my face....
>
> "He repeatedly called us she-asses, bitches, flies and swines and said: 'You were in the same beds with your husbands; why did you not prevent them from going out to do mischief? Now your skirts will be looked by the Police Constables'. He gave me a kick also and ordered us to undergo the torture of holding our ears by pass our arms round the legs, whilst being bent double.
>
> "This treatment was meted out to us in the absence of our men who were at the Bungalow."

Cowardice, thy name is Bosworth Smith! Moral degradation in a human being could not go any lower than this. Search the entire history of mankind, and you will fail to find the equal of this act in its ferocity and barbarism. How curious! The world believes still that England's mission in India is that of civilizing a backward people.

The Jallianwalla massacre and other "Punjab wrongs" gave a great impetus to the nationalist movement in India. What the Indian National Congress had failed to accomplish in its steady work of thirty-two years, the Punjab persecutions and humiliations did in the course of a few months. It has helped to arouse in the minds of the people of India a powerful national consciousness. It has been truly said that the blood of the martyrs at Jallianwalla Bagh has made the heart of all India to bleed.

Those who ask the question, "Why does India revolt?" may find a part of their answer in the word "Jallianwalla Bagh."

CHAPTER VIII

WHY IS INDIA POOR?

Only two hundred years ago India was the richest country in the world. Today it is the poorest. The gorgeous palaces of its kings with their enormous treasures were the objects of admiration and wonder for the other nations of the world. Its flourishing industries and its highly lucrative trade excited the greed and envy of the merchant classes everywhere. Its merchant ships laden with cargoes of valuable spices, silken and cotton manufactures, and precious jewels sailed into the harbors of England and other countries of Europe. How the maritime nations of the world vied with each other to possess the trade of the East Indies and fought over concessions in the Empire of the mighty Moghuls is a matter of common knowledge to all students of history. It was the fame of India that excited the imagination of Columbus when he set out westward on his historic voyage; it was only by accident that he discovered America. He had undertaken his voyage in search for a new route to the fabulous riches of India, so that America really owes her discovery to the fame of that ancient land. Pick up any standard work on mediæval history or classical literature and you will find that the riches of India and the splendor of the courts of its kings had become proverbial among the nations of Europe.

That fame of East Indian wealth which had inspired the careers of many a European explorer, military commander, and financial genius had totally disappeared long before the end of the nineteenth century; with the disappearing of the Indian kings the splendor of their courts had also vanished; with the extinction of the Indian fabric industries her flourishing trade had ceased; and simultaneously with the loss of its handicrafts and independence the prestige and prosperity of the nation had come to an end. As early as the year 1900 A.D. India had begun to be regarded by the historians as the poorest country in the world. Her daily per capita income was fixed at three quarters of a penny (equivalent to one and nine-sixteenths cents), and it was estimated that the dawn of the twentieth century found among the inhabitants of India one hundred and sixty million people who did not know what it was to have one square meal a day. The percentage of literacy, which included a knowledge of reading, writing, and arithmetic, had dropped from thirty-three per cent in 1757 to less than four per cent in 1900.

What is the cause of this astounding change in the condition of an ancient people like the East Indians? How did it happen that the same period which witnessed a sudden rise in the prosperity of most other nations of the world found in the Hindu nation an equal or even more sudden fall? What was the cause of the ruin of India's famous silk and cotton industries and of the loss of its political and economic independence? How did India drop from the highest rank to the lowest, from the proudest position to the humblest?

For this state of things in India writers have offered different explanations, several of which are so weak in nature that they would not stand even a superficial examination. The downfall of the country has been variously attributed to the low, immoral character of its populace and the selfishness and cowardice of their leaders, to a large increase in its population, to the inertia and extravagance of its agricultural class, to the rigorous caste system, and to the hatred and animosity which separates the different classes of its people. Some of these evils were responsible in some measure for the political downfall of India, but the reason for India's economic ruin must be sought for elsewhere. I maintain that the political subjugation of the country by England, and the pursuance by the latter of a fiscal policy dictated exclusively by the interests of British industries at the expense of the native claims, forms the basis of India's poverty and of its consequent "ills and woes."

We shall first examine, in order, the various reasons for the country's poverty which have been given by others, and which I believe to be unsatisfactory. Later I shall attempt to prove the truth of my thesis, that the cupidity of English financial and industrial lords has been the direct cause of India's ruin.

In the preceding pages much has been said concerning the moral character of the people of India. Those who have lived among them and have studied their habits and ideals at first hand know what heights of moral and spiritual purity the inhabitants of that ancient land once attained. Even in their present condition after generations of political subjection and economic poverty, both of which have a tendency to degrade the character of a people, it can be confidently said that the people of India, when measured by any moral, ethical, or cultural standard, will equal if not surpass any other people throughout the entire world. In order to judge the moral condition of this race at the time when their prosperity began to disappear, we shall let those speak who knew them at first hand.

Warren Hastings, whose name has been immortalized through his impeachment by Edmund Burke, had spent the best part of his life in India. Starting his career as a low-paid assistant of the East India Company, he had risen to the position of Governor-General of India. No one knew the people of that country better than did Warren Hastings, because of all foreigners he had the best opportunity to come in close contact with them. Yet he was no unqualified friend of India, as was fully disclosed during his impeachment by the House of Commons in England. Twenty-eight years after his retirement from India, Warren Hastings gave the following testimony before the British Parliament:

> "I affirm by the oath I have taken that this description of them [that the people of India were in a state of moral turpitude] is untrue and wholly unfounded.... They are gentle, benevolent, more susceptible of gratitude for kindness shown them than prompted to vengeance for wrongs inflicted, and as exempt from the worst

properties of human passion as any people on the face of the earth."[38]

It has been affirmed that overpopulation is the great cause of India's backwardness. But is India really over-populated? Has its population increased very largely during the last two hundred years? When we compare the census reports of the various countries of Europe, we find that several of them, England included, are more densely populated than India. If we compare England and India, we shall find that the increase in population in the latter has been no greater than that in the former since their political connection. In fact, since the beginning of the twentieth century the population of India has actually decreased, while that of England and several other countries of Europe has increased.

That the agricultural class of India is a race of thrifty, hard-working, abstemious, and experienced farmers who understand thoroughly the art of tilling the soil, has been attested by many foreigners, who had the opportunity to study their habits at close range. The quality of their knowledge of the farming profession and the extent of their initiative and perseverance may be judged from the achievements of Hindu farmers in California. Here was a class of agricultural people who had found it hard to make a decent living in the "land of five rivers," the Punjab. The Punjab is famous for its fertile soil and has an irrigation system which is regarded as the best in the world. Yet its agricultural population is in a state of semi-starvation because of top-heavy taxation and other unprogressive features of the country's administration. The moment these farmers from the Punjab were settled in the favorable environment of California they made a success of farming which is acknowledged by friends and foes alike. At the present time the anti-Asiatic laws of California prohibit Hindus from farming, but it is a matter of common knowledge that Hindu farm labor is paid higher wages in most sections than is American labor, because the Hindus are "steady," "hardworking," "informed," and "dependable."

Ignorance and sluggishness do not keep the Hindu farmer in a worse condition than is his own class in other countries; the small area of his holdings, excessive taxation, and lack of capital are continually dragging him backward. Eighty per cent of the people of India depend upon agriculture for their sole support. They live on the soil and by the soil. In former times India was also the home of flourishing cottage industries, that helped to increase the income of its enormous rural population. The invasion by English manufactures, caused by the selfish English fiscal policy for India, has completely uprooted the fabric industries of the Indian villages, a change which in turn has driven the entire people to the land for their livelihood, thereby bringing the total ruin of their economic prosperity.

Lack of moral stamina in the people, overpopulation, ignorance or sluggishness of the agricultural class are thus not the real causes of India's poverty. The economist who wishes to determine the cause of any country's poverty will have to ask himself the same questions which the Hindu historian, R. C. Dutt, asked in regard to India a quarter of century ago. "Does agriculture flourish? Are the finances properly administered, so as to bring back to the people an adequate re-

[38] Quoted from R. C. Dutt, *Economic History of British India*.

turn for the taxes paid by them? Are the sources of national wealth widened by a Government anxious for the welfare of the people?"

If it is true that in the same ratio as English power advanced in India economic prosperity of the country began to decline, we might as well inquire into the nature of British rule in India. We shall restrict our inquiry to the answers of the following two questions: "Why England acquired India?" and "Why England holds India?" It is a fact that England first came in contact with India through the medium of a trading company, whose object in establishing its trade stations in the Eastern country was profit-making. It is asserted that the British rulers of India have been guided in their work of governing the country by altruistic and humanitarian motives of a high quality. To what extent this claim of the English nation is founded on facts we shall examine presently. In any case such humanitarian principles as may have inspired the English rule in India, were of a much later origin. The primary reason for which England established its connections with its Eastern dependency was one of pure commercial greed. At the time when the East India Company was organized in England the people of Europe had not been trained in the use of such terms as "altruism" and "civilizing the backward peoples." These high-sounding epithets are products of much later times. The minds of the Directors of the East India Company were ruled by thoughts of large dividends and big profits.

The simple facts of the case are that the British went over to India as traders in order to make profit out of India. They found the people of that vast and prosperous country divided among themselves, and scenting the favorable opportunity, they set out cleverly to capitalize the weakness of the natives for their own gain. Yet according to the standards of the times nothing in their behavior was unusual or wrong. The world had never actually been ruled by altruism. The East India Company set the greedy, but innocent and confiding princes and peoples of India one against the other, and using the natives as their tools, became masters of the land. They have ever since held them under the lash as chattels and slaves, "hewers of wood and drawers of water" for Mother England. "Divide and rule" has been their constant motto. "Teach and liberate" has never crossed their minds. Such phrases have been invented by shrewd politicians merely to amuse and satisfy a class of idealistic people in England and abroad who fall innocent victims to artfully told lies. Such slogans were never intended as rules of state policy. Study carefully the tragic result of this long and laborious process of "liberating" a traditionally cultured and civilized people, and you will be convinced of the truth. The motto of "Divide and rule," on the other hand, they used mercilessly to emasculate a nation of helpless people, whom they made the innocent victims of their lust and greed. For the details of this early exploitation and "treading under foot" of the people of India read Edmund Burke's impeachment of Warren Hastings. Thus he closed his immortal condemnation of the barbarities of his own people on the soil of India:

> "I impeach Warren Hastings to high crimes and misdemeanors. I impeach him in the name of the Commons' House of Parliament, whose trust he has betrayed. I impeach him in the name of

the English nation, whose ancient honor he has sullied. I impeach him in the name of the people of India, whose rights he has trodden underfoot, and whose country he has turned into a desert. Lastly, in the name of every rank, I impeach the common enemy and oppressor of all!"

Mr. Wm. Digby, another Englishman, who lived in India for over twenty years as a member of the Indian Civil Service, gives valuable historical and economic data on the subject of English Imperialism in India, in his book ironically entitled *Prosperous British India*. The book is a scholarly work on history and economics and deserves the perusal of all thoughtful students. Mr. Digby shows that

1. Since the beginning of the English rule in the country the per capita income of the people of India has been gradually diminishing. The daily per capita income was

in 1850	2	pence
in 1880	1½	pence
in 1900	¾	pence.

2. That in 1900, proportionately to income, the Indian subject of the British Crown was taxed more than four times higher than was his Scottish fellow-subject, and three times higher than his English compeer. He quotes the following figures from the *Statesman's Yearbook*, 1900-1:

Proportion of Taxation to Income

Scotland with £45 per head as average, one-seventeenth	India (outside 1,000,000 well-to-do people) with 12s. per head as average, nearly one fourth.

3. In 1900 thirty-four and one-fifth days' income of every inhabitant of India was carried to England in the form of home charges. "Was ever such a crushing tribute exacted by any conqueror at any period of history?"

4. Since the British have been in the country famines have been more frequent, more widespread, and more deadly. "In the first quarter of the nineteenth century there were reported only four famines in the country, all of which were local. In the last quarter of the same century there occurred twenty-two famines which were general and spread all over the land."

A great nation was held a slave, was looted and routed, and yet the world never heard of such a thing as British injustice in India. But, let us ask, how was this great injustice perpetrated, this huge exploitation continued? This question is eminently sane and pertinent, and should be truthfully answered.

The English people were too intelligent not to profit by the experience of past conquerors and rulers over foreign races. As a result, they did not evidently hold India down, but they kept her down. First, they disarmed the natives totally. This procedure prevented armed rebellion, and the world was saved the news of consequent repressions. In other words, the English did not kill the people of India; they killed their spirit. They robbed them of their land and of their daily meals, and made them submissive and weak. The English novelist, Thackeray, described as follows the early stages of English rule in India:

> "It is very proper that, in England, a great share of the produce of the earth should be appropriated to support certain families in affluence, to produce senators, sages, and heroes for the service and the defense of the State, or, in other words, that great part of the rent should go to an opulent nobility and gentry, who are to serve their country in Parliament, in the army and navy, in the departments of science and liberal professions. The leisure, independence, and high ideas, which the enjoyment of this rent affords has enabled them to raise Britain to the pinnacle of glory. Long may they enjoy it;—but in India, that haughty spirit, independence, and deep thought, which the possession of great wealth sometimes gives, ought to be suppressed. They are directly adverse to our power and interest. The nature of things, the past experience of all governments, renders it unnecessary to enlarge on this subject We do not want generals, statesmen, and legislators; we want industrious husbandmen....
>
> "Considered politically, therefore, the general distribution of land, among a number of small proprietors, who cannot easily combine against Government, is an object of importance."

This policy was followed in India with unwavering resolution and fatal success.

It is an unfortunate fact of recorded history which no well-informed person may ignore, that under British rule the sources of national wealth in India have been narrowed in many ways. In the eighteenth century India was a great manufacturing as well as a great agricultural country. How its greatness disappeared totally, and it was left as a very poor agricultural country only, has been explained by many English and Indian writers. The decline of Indian industries has been attributed to the pursuance of a policy of commercial greed on the part of the British manufacturers. The English historian, H. H. Wilson, remarks:

> "The British manufacturer employed the arm of political injustice to keep down and ultimately strangle a competitor with whom he could not have contended on equal terms."[39]

We shall not tax the patience of our readers with irritating details of the ways in which this arm of political power was actually employed. But as a specimen we shall relate some of the incidents which helped to build the cotton fabric industry of England at the expense of India. It was the time of the home and cottage industries, when individuals or small groups of hand weavers owned their establishments and worked their business on a coöperative plan. The English merchants found they could not compete with the highly skilled and efficient Indian weavers; so they resolved to eliminate them altogether. This is what they did. The agents of the East India Company went to the village with the county magistrate (himself

[39] Quoted from R. C. Dutt.

an employee of the Company, because the Company was then the Government), and called together all the weavers of the village. The agent offered loans and advances to those weavers who would work for the Company. When the weavers refused to accept their offers, the agents of the Company forcibly tied the money in the napkins of the weavers, as a sign of their acceptance. The agents then drove the workers back to their homes until such time as the Company should demand their services. Thus they were forced to leave their own looms and to work in the Company's factories. There they were paid such low wages that many of them fled from their homes, and hundreds and thousands of others cut their thumbs and forefingers in order to render themselves immune from this forced labor.

By such means and others equally unfair "the prosperous class of Indian weavers was made tradeless and homeless, and many were driven into the jungle to starve and die." At the same time England completed the process of ruining the trade of India by charging an excise duty of 65% to 75% on Indian manufactures imported into England and admitting English-made goods into British India free of duty. These statements are not exaggerated. This procedure actually happened, and data gathered by the English themselves is freely available. But should the account be doubted when such and worse things happen in our own day everywhere?

All the high offices of governmental control, civil and military, were given over to Englishmen, and Indians were employed as menials and clerks. To be explicit: during the first one hundred and twenty-five years of British rule in India not one Indian sat on the provincial or national executive councils of the country. Until after the World War no Indian held the commission of a lieutenant colonel in the British army of India. If during this period India was not governed for the good of the Indians, it is no wonder. How full of meaning are the words of John Stuart Mill:

> "The government of a people by itself has a meaning and a reality; but such a thing as government of one people by another does not, and cannot exist. One people may keep another for its own use, a place to make money in, a human cattle-farm to be worked for the profits of its own inhabitants.
>
> "It is an inherent condition of human affairs that no intention, however sincere, of protecting the interests of others, can make it safe or salutary to tie up their hands. By their own hands only can any positive and durable improvement of their circumstances in life be worked out."[40]

Mr. Wm. Digby remarks on this account:

> "Thus England's unbounded prosperity owes its origin to her connection with India, whilst it has, largely, been maintained—disguisedly—from the same source, from the middle of the eighteenth century to the present time. 'Possibly, since the world began, no investment has ever yielded the profits reaped from the

[40] Quoted from R. C. Dutt.

Indian plunder' (Brooks Adams).

"What was the extent of the wealth thus wrung from the East Indies? No one has been able to reckon adequately, as no one has been in a position to make a correct tally of the treasure exported from India. Estimates have been made which vary from five hundred million pounds sterling to nearly one billion pounds sterling. Probably between Plassey (1757) and Waterloo the last-mentioned sum was transferred from Indian hoards to English banks.... Modern England has been made great by Indian wealth, wealth never proffered by its possessor, but always taken by the might and skill of the stronger. The difference between the eighteenth and twentieth centuries is simply that the amount received now is immensely larger and is obtained 'according to law'...."[41]

Let me quote Mrs. Sarojini Naidu, the "nightingale of India," as to the effect of British rule in India: "Our arts have degenerated, our literatures are dead, our beautiful industries have perished, our valor is done, our fires are dim, our soul is sinking."

All this has actually happened. Yet the world believes that England's mission in India is unselfish and holy, that she is there to save the souls of a demoralized people and to educate an ignorant and unprogressive nation. The nations have been made to believe that without her influence there would be social and religious tyranny in India, and that the weak would be left without a champion. The facts, however, read differently. The people are poor and weak. They are to a degree fanatic, and local conflicts occur occasionally between religious groups. But do the English rulers of India prevent these divisions or do they foster them? This is the important question.

The English are our masters. They make their laws as stringent as they please; they hold their grip as tight as they wish. They say to us: "People of India, you are weak. Weakness is recognized in our system as a crime. Therefore you are doomed." So they show the power in their hands and use it as they will. But when they say to us: "People of India, cease to quarrel and live in peace," they are not only cruel but unjust and hypocritical, for the quarrels are their own creation, and our divisions they recognize as their main support. Says the Premier of England, Mr. Ramsay MacDonald:

"As the red patches advanced over the map of India, sections pulled themselves together to resist, but no power then existing could develop that Indian cohesion which was necessary if the new trading invader was to be hurled back. We were not accepted, but we could not be resisted. India challenged, but could not make her challenge good.... Moreover, we were not a military conquering power imposing tribute and hastening hither and thither in our minds. The invasion was not of hordes of men seeking new settlements, nor of military captains seeking spoil, but of capital

[41] *Prosperous British India.*

> seeking investment, of merchants seeking profit. It was necessarily slow; it divided to rule, and enlisted Indians to subdue India."[42]

Perhaps the reader will now be ready to concede that England acquired control over India and has succeeded in holding her mastery over the country through the policy of "Divide and rule." He may grant also that the existing fabric industries of India have been destroyed by the unfair use of political power in the interest of the growing British manufactures. Then followed the invasion of the power loom in Europe which completed the ruin of India's cotton industry. In the first place India had been impoverished to such an extent that she could not find the necessary capital to utilize the latest inventions; and when at last she did succeed in setting up steam mills their progress was nipped in the bud through the imposition of an excise duty on all home manufactures. Here was an evident inversion of the natural order of things. When machinery began to be introduced into the country, a protective tariff was required to assist the infant industries. Instead, the foreign rulers of India imposed an excise duty on cotton fabrics, while foreign fabrics continued to be admitted free of duty.

A similar mischievous policy was adopted in regard to the agricultural industries of India. A government which has the welfare of the nation in mind tries in every way to improve the condition of the governed by increasing their sources of income. It grants its farmers subsidies, helps them to improve the quality of their crops, and extends their markets. What it exacts from them in the form of taxes is expended in the improvement of their general condition. "It identifies itself with the nation, and grows richer with it."

In India from the time when the East India Company became the rulers of the country, this natural process has been reversed. These foreign rulers of India regarded their possessions as a "human plantation," and their policy was to extract from the people all that was possible in order to swell the profits of the Company's stockholders in England. Taxes on agricultural land were placed at the highest possible point in the beginning, and were then increased at every successive revenue settlement. The over-assessment and collection of taxes with the most callous disregard for the material condition of the farmers, plunged the country into misery. Soon they began to flee from their houses into the jungles, leaving the country desolate. India was visited by the most horrible famines, and while natives died in the streets from hunger, the Company's agents had the gratification of reporting an increased collection from land taxes. It is estimated that the famine of 1770 carried away with it one-third of the entire population of Bengal, and yet in the following year the land revenue of Bengal was raised and actually collected in cash.

The two letters which were written from the Company's Government in India to its directors in England in the years 1771 and 1772 are of peculiar interest in this matter.

Dated 12th February, 1771: "Notwithstanding the great severity of the late famine and the great reduction of people thereby, some increase has been made in the settlements both of the Bengal and the Behar Provinces for the present year."[43]

[42] From *The Government of India.*

[43] Quoted from R. C. Dutt.

Dated 10th January, 1772: "The collections in each department of revenue are as successfully carried on for the present year as we could have wished."[44]

It is needless to say that in making a collection of an increased revenue, following a devastating famine, a great deal more ingenuity was needed. Every sort of advantage was taken of the distress of the people. Their crops were monopolized, and in most cases the seed for their next year's crops was sold to realize the Company's revenue. The hereditary owners of the lands were driven away from their holding, and their properties were transferred to the highest bidders for the land revenue collection.

A comparison between the land taxes claimed by the previous rulers of India and by the East India Company may be made from the following figures:

The total land revenue collected by the last Mohammedan ruler of Bengal in 1764, the last year of his administration, was £817,533; within thirty years the British rulers collected an annual land revenue of £2,680,000 in the same province. During this interval the country had been visited by two of the most terrible famines of its history. Colonel Briggs wrote in 1830: "A land tax like that which now exists in India, professing to absorb the whole of the landlord's rent, was never known under any Government in Europe or Asia."[45]

Aside from the heavy assessment of the Government there were, more disastrous still, the extortions and premiums of the Company's servants. Besides serving in the pay of the Company, each young clerk or old veteran officer was ambitious to make a sudden fortune to be carried with him to England. Nearly everyone of the Company's servants carried on his private trade. This evil was stopped, however, by Clive in later years. English traders used all the tools at hand to take improper advantage of their customers and of rival native traders.

A typical case of this injustice occurred during the controversy over excise duty in the Province of Bengal between its Nawab, Mir Kasam, and the Company's servants. The English victory at Plassey (1757) had greatly enhanced the prestige of the Company. In exchange for its protection, the Nawab of Bengal granted to the East India Company the right to carry on its export and import trade, free of duty, within his territory. This right the Nawab granted to the trade of the Company and not to the private trade of the officials of the Company. In spite of the repeated complaints from the Nawab, however, the Company's servants continued to carry on their private business without the payment of any duties into the treasury of the Nawab. This arrangement, of course, helped the private traders to rear colossal fortunes in a very short period, but the Nawab's treasury soon felt severely the loss of its revenue. Moreover, the suffering of the native merchants who had to pay heavy duties on their goods and thus found it difficult to compete with these law-breaking traders, reached a critical state. Overwhelmed from all sides, and finding his complaints to the Company's agents unheeded, the generous Nawab in a moment of noble and royal indignation abolished all inland duties. By this act he personally lost a large income from his revenues, but he placed his subjects on equal terms with the employees of the East India Company. What followed will

[44] Quoted from R. C. Dutt.

[45] Quoted from R. C. Dutt.

be scarcely believed by our readers. The Executive Council of the Company at Calcutta protested against this action of the Nawab as a breach of faith towards the English nation. "The conduct of the Company's servants upon this occasion," says James Mill in his history of India, "furnishes one of the most remarkable instances upon record of the power of interest to extinguish all sense of justice, and even of shame." "There can be no difference of opinion," writes another English historian, H. H. Wilson, "on the proceedings. The narrow-minded selfishness of commercial cupidity had rendered all members of the council, with the two honorable exceptions of Vansitart and Hastings, obstinately inaccessible to the plainest dictates of reason, justice and policy."[46] More comment upon this is unnecessary.

Here was a class of officials in India who regarded the country, which they had been called upon to govern in the name of God Almighty, as no other than a fishing pool. They declared that the purpose of their government was to restore order in place of chaos, and justice instead of corruption. But when one of the native princes, inspired by nobility of heart, ordered a cancellation of his own revenues in order to benefit his subjects, the government of the Company flared up in a rage and called his act of unselfish benevolence a breach of faith against the English nation. Edmund Burke was after all right when he spoke about the East India Company's officials thus:

> " ... The Tartar invasion was mischievous, but it is our protection that destroys India. It was their enmity, but it is our friendship. Our conquest there, after twenty years, is as crude as it was the first day. The natives scarcely know what it is to see the grey head of an Englishman; young men, boys almost, govern there without society, and without sympathy with the natives. They have no more social habits with the people than if they still resided in England; nor, indeed, any species of intercourse but that which is necessary to making a sudden fortune, with a view to a remote settlement. Animated with all the avarice of age, and all the impetuosity of youth, they roll in one after another, wave after wave, and there is nothing before the eyes of the natives but an endless, hopeless prospect of new flights of birds of prey and passage, with appetites continually renewing for a food that is continually wasting. Every rupee of profit made by an Englishman is lost forever to India" (Edmund Burke in a speech made in the House of Commons in 1783)."

After Plassey (1757) the English control over India began to expand rapidly, and the East India Company acquired the real nature of a government instead of a mere trading company. Gradually as the political power of the Company grew in India and abuses crept in, the English Parliament undertook to control all Indian affairs through appointed representatives. This policy was carried out in so far that on the eve of the Sepoy Mutiny (1857), which led to the transfer of the Government of India to the British Sovereign, the English Parliament already supervised the India affair through a cabinet minister and a council board in England, and a

[46] Quoted from R. C. Dutt.

governor-general appointed by the British cabinet in India.

The resentment of the people of India against the British rule and its consequent political and economic humiliations found its tragic expression in the rebellion of 1857, commonly known as the Sepoy Mutiny. The masses of the country led by the native army burst forth in mad fury against the yoke of their foreign rulers. The rebellion started in the United Provinces and at once spread like wildfire throughout the British territories. Once again the British played the natives against each other. The rebellion, which at one time threatened the complete overthrow of the British power in the country, was crushed with the assistance of Sikh regiments from Punjab. The suppression of the rebellion involved a terrible loss of life, and some of the deeds of horror which were committed by the infuriated English soldiery remain as fresh in the minds of the Indian people to this day as they were in 1857. The last of the Moghul emperors was deposed and all of his heirs were fired from the mouths of cannon. Thousands of rebels were hung, and their dead bodies were left hanging from the branches of trees in order to excite terror in the minds of the populace. Kaye and Malleson's *History of the Mutiny* gives the most horrible account of the butchery which the English officers carried on during the bloody days after the Mutiny in the most indiscriminate and barbarous fashion. The authors of this memorable account of the Mutiny state: "Already our military officers were hunting down the criminals of all kinds, and hanging them up with as little compunction as though they had been pariah-dogs, or jackals, or vermin of a baser kind." So ferocious was the temper of the white soldiers, and so strongly had the fierce hatred against all "who wore the dusky livery of the East" possessed them, that on one occasion in the absence of tangible enemies they turned on their own camp-followers and murdered a large number of their loyal and unoffending servants. Sir Charles Ball writes: "Every day we had expeditions to burn and destroy disaffected villages and we had taken our revenge. We have the power of life in our hands and I assure you, we spare not." Innocent old men and helpless women with sucking infants at their breasts felt the weight of the white man's vengeance just as much as the vilest malefactors. It is recorded that in several places cow's flesh was forced by spears and bayonets into the mouths of Hindu prisoners because the English knew that the Hindu so abhors cow's flesh that he will rather die than eat it. Kaye and Malleson write:

> "Afterwards the thirst for blood grew stronger still. It is on the records of our British Parliament, in papers sent home by the Governor-General of India in Council, that the aged, women and children, are sacrificed, as well as those guilty of rebellion. They were not deliberately hanged, but burnt to death in their villages—perhaps now and then accidentally shot. Englishmen did not hesitate to boast, or to record their boastings in writings, that they had 'spared no one', and that 'peppering away the niggers' was very pleasant pastime, 'enjoyed amazingly'. It has been stated in a book patronized by high class authorities, that 'for three months eight dead-carts daily went their rounds from sunrise to sunset to take down the corpses which hung at crossroads and

> market-places', and that 'six thousand beings' had been thus summarily disposed of and launched into eternity."[47]

Following the Sepoy Mutiny an act was passed in the British Parliament by virtue of which the government of India was transferred from the East India Company to the British Crown. The English King thus became the ruler of India, but the people of India paid the price of purchase. The shareholders of the Company were recompensed for this change, and the amount paid to them was added to the national debt of India. The government of the country changed hands, but virtually no change was made in the policy. Even in the times of peace that followed the public debt of India continued to increase. The new rulers were determined to promote English industries at the expense of Indian manufacturers just as had been done under the rule of the Company. India remained henceforth a colony of the Empire for the production of raw materials at very low prices in the English factories. The manufactured goods were afterwards re-shipped to India for the native consumption. The posts of dignity and high emolument in the government service continued to be regarded by the Englishman as his sole monopoly. No confidence was placed in the natives; they were given no positions of authority, and were excluded from offices of responsibility as much as possible. In other words, the interests of Indians were completely subordinated to those of the Englishmen. "The roads to wealth and honor were closed to the natives. The highest among them were considered unworthy of those places of trust in the state employments which were held by young English boys fresh from school. The springs of Indian industry were stopped, and the sources of the country's wealth were dried up."

As a result of the direct British rule over India the public debt of the country rose from £51,000,000 in 1857 to £200,000,000 in 1901. The agricultural class of India, moreover, the backbone of national prosperity in a country whose main occupation is agriculture, had become so poor that in one district in 1900 85% of the land revenue was directly paid to the Government officials by money-lenders, the landowners being wholly unable to meet their obligations. It was estimated by the leading medical journal of the world (*The Lancet*, June, 1901) that during the last decimum of the nineteenth century nineteen millions of British Indian subjects had died of starvation, and one million from plague. And yet at the beginning of the twentieth century according to the financial arrangements of the country half of its total revenue was sent out of India to England each year. This included the upkeep of the India office in London, pensions to retired officials residing in England, and interest on public debts.[48]

With these facts in mind the reader will not wonder that India is poor. Place any other country in the world under the same conditions. Let her government be carried on by a foreign power with the complete exclusion of the sons of the soil from positions of responsibility; let her fiscal policy be determined by the parliament of a rival commercial nation without a single representative of the governed nation sitting in its councils; let its industry be crippled or destroyed by a malicious use of political power by its foreign rulers; let its agriculture be subjected to

[47] Quoted from Lajpat Rai.
[48] Digby.

a heavy and uncertain land tax; let half its total revenue be carried away annually to a foreign land; and you will not be surprised if the most prosperous nation in the world sinks in the course of a few years to the lowest depths of poverty and degradation.[49]

A nation prospers if its government is wisely administered in the interest of the people, if the sources of wealth are widened, and if the proceeds from taxation are spent for the uplift of the people and among the people. It is impoverished if its government is carried on by an outside power for the purpose of exploitation; if the sources of its wealth are narrowed from the crippling of its industries, and if its revenues are largely remitted out of the country without an economic return. Americans stand in awe before the single monopoly of the Standard Oil Company. They are appalled by the magnitude and tyranny of its power. They should remember that the Standard Oil monopoly is a pigmy before the British monopoly of India. England has exercised for nearly two hundred years exclusive and undivided control over the affairs of India. She has had power to shape the destinies of three hundred million people according to her will, being responsible to no one but herself. She has held not only the government of India, but its commerce, its finances, and its industry. In conclusion let us repeat the poignant remark quoted earlier, "The national wealth of India did not sprout wings and fly away. It had to be carried away."

[49] Digby.

CHAPTER IX

INDIAN NATIONALISM—ITS ORIGIN AND GROWTH

Before discussing at length the problems of Indian nationalism, let us consider whether India is really a nation, or is merely a composite of peoples inhabiting the same country. India's fundamental unity as a nation has been denied often by prominent scholars, while its historic and cultured oneness has really never been acknowledged by the English rulers of the country. Sir John Strachey remarks:

> "This is the first and most essential thing to learn about India—that there is not and never was an India, or even any country of India, possessing, according to European ideas, any sort of unity, physical, political, social, or religious; no Indian nation, no 'people of India' of which we hear so much."

We believe that Sir John Strachey is profoundly wrong in his assertion that India is not a nation in the "physical, political, social, or religious" sense. On the contrary, it can be proved easily that geographically, historically, culturally, and spiritually India is fundamentally one. Cut off from the north and the east by the snow-clad Himalayas, and surrounded on the south and the west by the mighty Indian Ocean, India is geographically, one country. Every part of the interior is freely accessible from all sides. No natural boundary lines within the country divide it into different parts; nor do any high mountains obstruct the free passage from one part of the country to the other. In fact, India is a physical unit, much more distinct than any other country in Europe or America.

When we study the history of India, from the ancient Vedic period to modern times, we find again the whole of the Indian peninsula, from Bengal to Gujrat, and from Ceylon to Kashmir, mentioned always as one motherland. "The early Vedic literature contains hymns addressed to the Motherland of India. The epic poems speak of the whole of BHARAT as the home-land of Aryans." We hear nowhere any account of separate nationalities within the country. The literature of India is full of thoughts about Indian nationality; but there is no mention of separate Bengal, Madras, Gujrat, or Punjab nations, based upon geographic divisions. Powerful emperors in ancient as well as modern times have ruled over the entire peninsula in peace and security. "In fact, the belief in the unity of India was so strong in ancient times that no ruler considered his territories complete until he had acquired control over the entire peninsula." Asoka ruled over the whole of India in perfect harmony. Akhbar's power spread to the farthest ends of the land.

And when, later on, the different governors of the border provinces rose in revolt and refused allegiance to the successors of Akhbar, it was the great distance from the capital that suggested revolt to the population of these distant provinces, and not a feeling of separate nationality.

Culturally, again, India is one nation. In their daily habits, their ethical standards, and their spiritual responses the Indians of every religion and locality are fundamentally alike. "Their family life is founded on the same bases; their modes of dress and cooking are the same. Their very tastes are similar." They respect the same national heroes and worship the same ideals. They have the same hopes and aspirations in this life and in the hereafter. As a result, their mental and spiritual behavior is similar. In fact, they are fundamentally one in mind and in spirit.

It is true that more than one dialect is spoken in the country. Until 1920 the business of the Indian National Congress itself was carried on in the English language because no other language was common to the whole of India. It was really tragic that a people who were so profoundly proud of their national heritage and who aspired to political freedom were obliged to use at the meetings of their national assemblies an utterly foreign language. That the variety of languages was in fact a very slight difficulty was demonstrated at the session of the Indian National Congress in 1920. From the Congress platform at Amritsar in 1919 Mahatma Gandhi had announced that at all subsequent meetings the business of the Congress would be conducted in the Hindi language, which is spoken by more than a third of the population of the country. Teachers were sent immediately to different parts of the country to instruct the people in the Hindi language and when the Congress convened again in 1920 its business was carried on in Hindi. Delegates from Bengal, Madras, and Bombay made their speeches in Hindi as fluently as those from the United Provinces and the Punjab. Every one felt satisfied at the change. A miracle had happened; *India had acquired a common tongue in the course of a year*.

The population of India is composed of many different peoples, who came to the country originally as invaders, and later settled there and became a part thereof. Through the process of assimilation and adaptation extending over generations, the original Afghan, Mongol, and Persian conquerors of India have lost their peculiar characteristics, and become one with the rest of the population in their language, ideas, and loyalties. The position of these foreign types in India is exactly analogous to peoples of different nationalities, who migrated from Europe into America in the early times. The interval of a single generation was usually sufficient to transfer the loyalties of European immigrants from their native countries to the United States. The difference between India and the United States in this respect is merely that the Indian must go back many more generations to reach his immigrant than must the American.

The chief barrier in the way of spiritual unity among the people of India, is religion. Hinduism and Mohammedanism are the dominant religions of the country. The main portion of the population is Hindu, but seventy millions of Mohammedans are scattered over the whole country in small groups. The Mohammedans came to India originally as invaders and conquerors, and now occupy a position in the country of mixed authority and subjection. Wherever they form the majority group, they dominate the followers of other religions; while in other places they are held down as minorities. Since the beginning of their contact the Hindus and the Mohammedans of India have never agreed. Intervals of peace and harmony between the two communities have occurred occasionally during the reigns of benevolent emperors like Akhbar and Shah Jahan; but their hearts were never joined in true companionship even before the beginning of English influence. The modern rulers of India have helped to strengthen the differences between the Hindus and the Mohammedans in so far that the animosities between the two religious groups were no less bitter in 1918 than they were three hundred years ago. Since the days of Gandhi's leadership, however, a great deal has been accomplished in building up a feeling of genuine comradeship and love between the Hindus and Mohammedans of India. When the Moslems all over the world were in a state of deep distress at the Khilafat issues after the Severes treaty, the Hindus of India made common cause with the Moslems of the world. Khilafat was included in the Congress program as one of India's main issues. This liberality helped to win the hearts of the Mohammedan population of India toward their Hindu compatriots, and the Hindu Gandhi was idolized by both religious groups, as leader and savior. It was an auspicious beginning of friendship between these two isolated factions in India, and ever since it has been enthusiastically followed up by the younger generation of the country. It may be confidently expected that as the youth of India acquire influence in the affairs of the country, the friction between the Hindus and the Mohammedans will cease, and their age-long battles based upon superstition and error will come to an end.

Worse still in their ethical and spiritual significance are the differentiations between the caste groups among the Hindus. Numerous social reform societies are working at the present time to remove the barriers of caste within Hindu society; and until the work of building up a human fellowship among the different caste and religious groups of India, based upon the highest moral teachings of the Hindu sages, is completed, the political as well as spiritual regeneration of the country will remain an idle dream.

We have seen that in the cultural sense, on account of the sameness of feelings and instincts, the Hindus, Mohammedans, Sikhs, Parsis, Bengalis, Mahratas, and Madrasis are fundamentally alike. Yet the bitterness between these warring elements of the country had grown into such immense proportions at one time that a communal feeling of neighborhood and human decency among them seemed inconceivable. Two hundred years ago, when the English first began to acquire control over the country, the people of India were divided into perfectly hostile groups; and no power then existed which could bring together these warring factions. Among the causes that have secretly conspired to develop a spirit of unity among the different religious and social groups of India, the foremost has been British imperialism in the country. Britain gave to India, in the first place, a long reign of peace. This enabled the people of different parts of the country to have a more direct and steady intercourse than was possible in earlier times. The English also gave to the higher classes of India a knowledge of English history and classical literature, whose study breathed into the minds of the educated Indians a love of liberty. Acquaintance with the spirit of European nationalism created a desire for Indian nationality. A national consciousness soon sprang into existence and found expression through the medium of the Indian National Congress.

Greater than everything else, however, in its direct consequences of uniting the people of India into one nation has been the universal antagonism toward British rule. As the tyranny of foreign rule gradually began to be felt, hatred against it increased. The different factions in the country were forced to unite for the purpose of driving out of the country the arrogant intruders. Whatever else may be doubtful, one thing is certain about India: "The sentiment of antagonism toward British rule and of resentment against its iniquitous character is both universal and profound."

The principal grievances against English rule are its alien character and its exploitation of the country's wealth. Mahatma Gandhi calls it "Satanic," because it is founded not upon the consent of the governed but upon the military strength of the ruler. "It is based not on right but on might. Its last appeal is not to reason or to the heart but to the sword." Gandhi writes:

> "I came reluctantly to the conclusion that the British connection had made India more helpless than she ever was before, politically and economically.... The government established by law in British India is carried on for this exploitation of the masses. No sophistry, no jugglery in figures can explain away the evidence the skeletons in many villages present to the naked eye. I have no doubt whatsoever that both England and the town-dwellers of India will have to answer, if there is a God above, for this crime against humanity which is perhaps unequalled in history."—Gandhi, *Speeches*, pp. 753-4.

We said just now that one of the main grievances against English rule in India is its alien character. It may be asked: "Why should the alien origin of a rule itself be such a strong argument against it?" "Is it not true that England has given to India peace and efficiency in government? That constitutes the chief function of governments everywhere, and the rule which has successfully achieved this purpose justifies its existence. If it is true elsewhere, it should be true in India also." Our questioner may be both profoundly right and profoundly wrong. However, the acceptance or rejection of a foreign lordship by the heart is a matter of such subtle sentiment, that the only way to explain its meaning to the reader is to create a situation where he shall be called upon to judge in the matter.

Let us suppose that by some trick of fortune Japan obtained mastery over America. Let us grant, at the same time, that the Japanese rule over America was more efficient than the American rule, and in the light of our modern knowledge it is not beyond the limit of probability to imagine that Japanese efficiency in government could be greater than American efficiency. How would our reader feel about the situation? Would he be willing to discard his own indigenous native government for the sake of a more efficient rule under the Japanese Mikado? What would be his reaction if he saw his own "stars and stripes" replaced by the Imperial flag of Japan? Certainly, he would not feel at ease about the matter. The condition of the native of India under British authority is exactly similar in cause and consequence. In its fundamental aspect the rule of a country by an alien power is essentially wrong in principle. It is unnatural and hence utterly immoral. Whether it is the Japanese in Korea, the United States of America in the Philippine Islands, or the English in India—it is all unnatural and immoral. There can never be any ethical, moral, or spiritual justification of an other than native rule in a country. "The government of a people by itself," says John Stuart Mill, "has a meaning and reality; but such a thing as government of one people by another does not, and cannot exist."

So far there have existed only two principles for the government of any country in the world, one is the government of a country by its chosen representatives, who are held responsible to their constituents, and are necessarily required to rule the country in the interests of the governed. This system was described by an American emancipator as "government of the people, by the people, for the people." When we look back over the histories of the different countries of the world, we find that, without a single exception, the countries which have advanced in their material and cultural possessions, during the past two hundred years, have been those whose governments were based on the principle of "government of the people, by the people, for the people."

In the modern world we find that the governments of the United States of America, England, France, and Germany are typical for their representative characters. It goes without saying that the progress which these nations have made during recent times would not have been possible under any other system of government. Take the case of any of these countries, America for example; you will find that "America has been made great by the democratic character of its governmental institutions. Its colossal achievements in the mechanical arts, the high advancement in its cultural and artistic life, the mammoth nature of its commercial and industrial progress, the magnitude of its educational equipment, its institutions of learning and research, and its high standard of living—all these owe their origin to the beneficent character of the American government," whose foundation was laid upon the noble principles contained in the Declaration of Independence:

> " ... That all men are created equal; That they are endowed by their Creator with certain inalienable rights; that among these are life, liberty, and the pursuit of happiness. That, to secure these rights, governments are instituted among men, deriving their just powers from the consent of the governed; ..."

There is still another principle (or lack of principle) on which the government of a country could be based. This occurs where the country is governed by an alien power, which derives its authority not from the consent of the governed, but from some outside source. As a natural consequence of this system the rulers of such countries are not concerned with the benefits to be derived by the ruled country. In such cases the interests of the subject nation are completely subordinated to those of the master country. "The commerce of the ruling power is expanded at the expense of the ruled; the industries of the governing country are enhanced at the cost of the extinction of those of the governed." "The material, cultural, and moral life of one people is enriched at the expense of the life sources of a more helpless and unfortunate people." The process begins with the impoverishing of the subject nation through a system of economic exploitation of its wealth resources by the dominant powers. Poverty in its turn degrades the character of the people, and the nation becomes morally flabby. The degeneration of an impoverished and suppressed people is assisted by the deteriorating influence of the other policies of the foreign ruler, such as the disarming of the subject people, the introduction in their midst of an alien system of education so designed as to form in its higher classes a group of miseducated "snobs" and to create in the upper sections of the country contempt for its past history and culture.

This kind of government has existed in India for the past two hundred years. To begin with, England carried away all the tangible wealth of the country "in the form of indemnities, grants, and gifts from its princes, and assessments and taxes from the people." At the same time the industries of the country were destroyed, and its commercial prosperity was checked by a selfish policy of enriching the manufacturing classes of England at the expense of those in India. The entire population of the country was disarmed as the next step. Thus were the natures of the people degraded, their martial spirit was crushed, and "a race of soldiers and heroes converted into a timid flock of quill-driving sheep."

The introduction of an utterly alien system of education was still another step in rooting out of the country the remnants of national honor and pride. According to the scheme of English education in the country, formulated by Lord Macaulay, English was made the medium of instruction for all branches of study. English history and English literature received preference over Indian history and Indian literature. The text-books for schools and colleges were prepared by English agents of the government; and from them sentiments of love and admiration for Indian civilization and culture on one hand, and respect for the character and behavior of its princes on the other, were rigidly excluded. In its place the English kings, the English people, the English religion, the English government, the English institutions, in fact everything English was held up as ideal. According to the history texts, whenever a battle was fought between the English and the native princes, the former were always in the right and the latter forever in the wrong. The English were always the victorious, and the natives always the beaten party. Mir Jafar, the arch-traitor of the country, was a noble and worthy prince, while Mir Kasam, the benevolent protector of his subjects against the injustice of the East India Company's agents, was a hypocrite and a debauché. The reason for the exaltation of Mir Jafar and the execration of Mir Kasam is, however, easily understood. Mir Jafar was the commander-in-chief of the army of Siraj-ud-Daulah, who stood against the forces of Lord Clive on the battlefield of Plassey. At a suggestion of bribery from Clive, Mir Jafar led the whole of his army over to the side of the enemy, and thus secured for the English the victory of Plassey, which was the beginning of their real power in the country. On the other hand, Mir Kasam was continually fighting against the encroachments of the East India Company over his own territories and the rights of his subjects. Which of the two princes was a real man and a worthy hero among his people, Mir Jafar or Mir Kasam? Mir Kasam, according to every kind of moral and ethical standard of nobility and courage; Mir Jafar, according to the corrupt standards of British Imperialism in India.

After the Indian youths had finished their scanty education, the future that lay before them was of a very uninviting nature. As all the high offices in the service of the country were monopolized by the English, the only positions left for the educated classes of Indians were those of low-paid clerks and assistants in the government offices. No prospect of fame, or wealth, or power opened before them. There was no great stimulus for the pursuit of higher knowledge. The young scholars no sooner began to know their positions in the world than they realized the uselessness of great attainments. Of what use was their learning if they were not to have employment as responsible public administrators of their country and so use their knowledge in the service of India? The extent of the exclusion of the native inhabitants of the country from offices of dignity and high emoluments in the government service may be realized from the following figures. According to the figures of 1913, out of 2,501 civil and military offices in British India carrying monthly salaries of 800 rupees ($266.00) or more, only 242, less than ten per cent were held by Indians; out of the 4,986 appointments carrying a monthly salary of 500 rupees ($166.00), only 19 per cent were held by Indians; and out of the 11,064 appointments carrying a monthly salary of 200 rupees ($66.00) only 42 per cent were held by Indians. Conditions have not changed much since 1913.[50]

In order to enable the American reader to realize fully the magnitude of injustice involved in the wrong policies of the English government in India regarding the country's systems of education and public employment, we shall use our previous illustration once more. Let it be supposed that simultaneously with the consolidation of Japanese power in America it was ordered by the Mikado that henceforth the Japanese language should form the sole medium of instruction in the schools and colleges throughout the United States. The American children would be required to learn the Japanese language before reaching school. The texts given to the youths of the country to study and digest would be books written and published in Japan, from which the names of such national heroes as Washington and Lincoln were excluded, but in which the praises of Japan were sung in high chorus. Shakespeare, Milton, Emerson, Longfellow, and Hawthorne would be excluded from the American school curriculum, and Japanese literature substituted in its place. The business of all governmental departments would be conducted in Japanese, and its official circulars and reports would be printed in Japanese. All the higher posts in the service of the country would be reserved for the Mikado's own countrymen. The president and his cabinet; supreme, district, and superior court judges; the governors of the states,—all would be appointed in Tokyo from among the Japanese in favor with the government of the Mikado. Native-born Americans would be employed only as stenographers, postmen, grammar school teachers, and street car conductors, and then only at starvation wages. Buddhism would be made the state religion of America. What would any self-respecting American say

[50] Quoted from Lajpat Rai.

if all this were done to his country? What would he do when his children and his grandchildren raised a cry against the injustice done to their country and its manhood, and this cry was drowned by the declaration of the Japanese imperialists that Japan was carrying the Yellow Man's burden in the United States of America.

The feeling of a deep and passionate resentment felt by the people of India regarding these matters was expressed by the late Mr. G. K. Gokhale thus:

> "A kind of dwarfing or stunting of the Indian race is going on under the present system. We must live all our lives in an atmosphere of inferiority, and the tallest of us must bend, in order that the exigencies of the system may be satisfied. The upward impulse, if I may use such an expression, which every schoolboy at Eton or Harrow may feel, that he may one day be a Gladstone, a Nelson, or a Wellington, and which may draw forth the best efforts of which he is capable, that is denied to us. The height to which our manhood is capable of rising can never be reached by us under the present system. The moral elevation which every Self-Governing people feel, cannot be felt by us. Our administrative and military talents must gradually disappear owing to sheer disuse, till at last our lot, as hewers of wood and drawers of water in our own country, is stereotyped."

If, therefore, the world sees the spectacle of an indignant India in revolt against the English rule, it should not be surprised. It is only natural that the English should resent the attempts of the Indians to secure their independence. It is hoped, however, that the other nations of the world will not feel hostile against the battle cry of the Indians against the British oppression in their country. If the English imperialists try to prove the virtue of their rule in India, please remember that the question is not whether the English rule is good or bad, but whether the principle underlying it is right or wrong. No self-respecting American citizen desires to see Japanese lordship established in his native land; he would call a condition intolerable in which the Japanese held all the positions of power in the government of his country. The full-blooded inhabitants of India feel in much the same way about the British supremacy in India. The reason of this attitude of both American and Indian nationalists is the same. The self-respect of an honest man revolts against foreign domination. The eyes of Modern India have been opened, and her people realize "that they are men, with a man's right to manage his own affairs." As was expressed by Mrs. Annie Besant in her presidential address before the Indian National Congress in 1917: "India is no longer on her knees for 'boons'; she is on her feet for Rights."

The first voice of organized Indian nationalist opinion demanding reform in the British government of India, was heard in 1885. In that year the first session of the Indian National Congress was held in Bombay. The Congress began as a gathering of a small group of progressive nationalist leaders from different parts of the country. Gradually, as its function became known, the ranks of the congress were swelled by delegates from all sections of India, and soon its responsible character as the representative organ of Indian progressive opinion on political matters was recognized in both England and India.

The Congress began its career as a critic of British policies in the country. It submitted a request to the English nation for an inquiry into Indian affairs and presented claims for reforms in the irresponsible and autocratic character of the British Government in the country. As time passed and the real nature of English rule began to be disclosed, the Indian nationalists became "bolder in their criticisms and more ambitious in their claims for reform." Except for minor concessions granted through the courtesy of a few sympathetic viceroys nothing positive in the direction of the better government of India was accomplished by the Indian National Congress until the Morley-Minto reforms of 1909. Yet in spite of its enormous difficulties, arising from the stubbornness of British bureaucracy in India and the cold, unconcerned attitude of the English Parliament towards Indian claims, the Congress had done excellent work in arousing the educated classes of the country to a realization of their political wrongs.

The Indian nationalist movement received a great impetus during the harsh reign of Lord Curzon as the high-handed Viceroy of India. One of the acts of Lord Curzon was the partition of Bengal in 1905,—"an act which aroused in the entire population of Bengal a violent outburst of popular disapproval." The purpose of the English Viceroy in dividing the province into two portions was to destroy the unity of Bengal, and to sow at the same time seeds of bitter Hindu-Muslim feuds. But the Bengalee youths were determined not to accept the dismemberment of their ancient land of Bengal, and the entire province was in a state of anarchy for a period of six years. In spite of the attempts of the English to quiet the agitation, it gradually spread all over India until at last the hated act was repealed by royal proclamation at the Delhi coronation Durbar in 1911.

In the meantime the Morley-Minto reforms, sponsored by John Morley, the noted biographer of Gladstone and at that time Secretary of State for India, and Lord Minto, the Viceroy of India, had become law by the India Council Act of 1909. The reforms were accepted by a few moderate leaders as "generous," but on the whole public opinion in India regarded them as inadequate and petty. For the first time seats in the executive councils of the provinces as well as those in the Indian government were thrown open to Indians. The provincial and central legislative councils were enlarged and made to include more "elected" Indian members. Henceforth the provincial councils were to contain a majority of "non-official" "elected" members as distinguished from the "official" and "non-official nominated" members, the official being the officers of the Government who sat in the councils as ex-officio members and the non-official nominated who were nominated to their positions as council members by the governor of the province for provincial councils and by the Viceroy in the case of the central council.

The powers of the reformed councils, however, were limited. "The councils," says Prof. Parker T. Moon, "could pass resolutions subject to the British Parliament's overriding authority; they could discuss the budget and other measures; they could criticise and suggest. They could not oppose and propose, but neither depose nor dispose. They could not overthrow the administration, or tighten the purse strings. They were, in short, experimental debating clubs."[51]

Those who had put their confidence in the Morley-Minto reforms were soon disappointed. The real nature of the new councils as mere "debating clubs" was discovered and found unsatisfactory. The people of India had demanded the right to control the affairs of their country's government, and they had been granted merely the right to discuss and to criticize, with no authority whatsoever to alter the policies of its officials. The helplessness of the Indian members in the Councils was proved after the World War during the agitation over the Rowlatt Bills. The uproar against this piece of repressive legislation was so strong that all Indian members of the Central Legislative Council, including those who were nominated by the government, voted against its passage. But in spite of the solid opposition from Indian members in the Council and an unprecedented revulsion against the Bills among all classes in the country, they were made law by the Viceroy. That legislation was a "direct slap in the face of nationalist India." It is a matter of common knowledge that it led to the *satyagraha* of Mahatma Gandhi, which in turn crystallized into the non-violent non-coöperation movement.

After the reforms of 1909, the Indian National Congress continued to arouse the masses of the country to a national consciousness and to a demand for representation in the government of the country. In 1914 all groups of Indians joined in a spirit of loyalty to assist the British Empire during the World War. India made heavy contributions to the war-time needs of England in both man-power and money power; as a recompense for her loyalty the people of India were promised liberal home rule after the war. In the meantime the Indian National Congress and the All-India Moslem League (founded in 1912 by the Mohammedans of India) had agreed to present the joint claims of all communities in the country for home rule. The scheme formulated by these two organizations at Lucknow in 1916, and known as the Congress-League Scheme, had for its aim the attainment of *Swaraj* (home rule) within the British Empire. They proposed a plan by which India within a period of fifteen years should acquire the same rights as the self-governing colonies of the Empire.

Before the end of the war, the Secretary of State for India, Mr. Montague, was sent to India by the British Parliament for the study of the conditions of the country with a view to launching a scheme of wider influence for its people. A joint report prepared by the Secretary, Mr. Montague, and the Viceroy, Lord Chelmsford, was published in 1918, and after slight modifications was passed by the British Parliament as the Act of 1919.

Although the Montague-Chelmsford reforms were an improvement over the reforms of 1909, all sections of the Indian people except a few isolated moderates at once declared them to be unsatisfactory. Besides enlarging the existing councils and providing for more elected members in them, the reforms of 1919 introduced the new principle of "dyarchy" into the provinces. The various departments of the provincial government were known as "reserved" or "transferred." The control of the "reserved" departments remained in the hands of the governors, who were not responsible in any way to the legislatures. These included law, order, justice,

[51] *Imperialism and World Politics*, page 300.

and police. The class of "transferred" subjects included among others education, agriculture, and public health. Their control was placed in the hands of ministers elected by and responsible to the provincial legislatures, which contained a majority of elected members. The system of "dyarchy" in the provincial governments, however, was not a success. No sooner had the new scheme begun to function than difficulties over the budget arose between the ministers in charge of different departments. The ministers of transferred subjects were given the privilege of managing their departments according to popular demand, but they were not provided with the funds necessary to make possible the proposed reforms. "The strings of the purse were still held by an outside power," a condition which made work of these responsible ministers wholly ineffective. "In defiance of Lincoln's principles regarding the fate of a house divided against itself," comments Prof. Moon, "the British Government made it a principle to divide the administration of India. India was to be 'half free, half slave.' Autocracy and self-government were to be twin columns supporting British imperialism. It is interesting to note the subjects which were reserved as of interest to Great Britain—the repression of disorder was a prime interest. Ingenious as it was, the scheme was by no means an unqualified success."[52]

Yet it must be admitted that the reforms of 1919 were never given a fair trial by the people of India. Before the time came for the installation of the new councils, the Indian nation had already launched upon its career of non-violent non-coöperation against the British Government. How the agitation against the Rowlatt Bills led to martial law in the Punjab and to the massacre at Amritsar, which in turn drove Mahatma Gandhi and the Indian National Congress to the policy of boycott against English rule, has already been explained in a previous chapter. One of the items in the non-coöperation program of the Congress was the boycott of councils, and as a consequence of this item all the responsible nationalist leaders withheld their names and support from the council elections. When after the arrest of Mahatma Gandhi in 1922, one wing of the Indian nationalists under the leadership of Mr. C. R. Das, decided to go into the councils, they did so with the purpose of breaking them up. The avowed object of followers of Mr. Das, who were henceforth called the "Swarajists," was to capture the councils with a view to breaking the machinery of the government from within by obstructing its business at every step. Even though the "Swarajists" finally did succeed in holding the majority seats in different legislative councils of the country, and in causing considerable annoyance to the government officials by their obstructionist methods, yet they were far from being able at any time to halt the government machinery.

The point at issue between India and England is this: India has outgrown its old habit of submission. It does not bend its knee to beg for reforms and concessions. It is standing on its feet and demanding its rights, and the methods it is using to secure the rights of the people to govern themselves are of its own creation. The surprising thing in this whole affair is not that India has lost faith in the British sense of justice and has decided to boycott its English rulers; the amazing thing is that it took the people of India so long to find out the truth about England's inter-

[52] *Imperialism and World Politics,* page 303.

ests in the country and their own welfare. It is a sad commentary upon the genius of Indian leadership that it took the Indian National Congress thirty-five years to discover the path of non-coöperation towards *Swaraj* (home rule). To expect from the English nation, which rewarded General Dyer for his massacre of 800 unarmed civilians with a purse of £10,000 ($50,000), a grant of self-government was stark nonsense. And yet until the new path was struck out by Mahatma Gandhi in 1920, Indians of all shades of opinion persevered in their belief that freedom could be acquired by begging. Mahatma Gandhi was the first man among Indians to realize the fact that freedom is never got by gifts of the rulers, but on the contrary is won by the might of the ruled. Freedom is a thing which cannot be given to a nation from outside; the ability to acquire it must be developed from within.

It is really amazing how old habits stick with beings long after their uselessness has been established. A case of this occurred in India after the incarceration of Mahatma Gandhi in 1922. The Mahatma had started the country on the lines of non-coöperation, and they were proceeding quite successfully, when he was suddenly arrested and sentenced to six years' imprisonment. Soon after he had disappeared from the scene of the Congress, there sprang up in its midst a new party which at once resolved to go back into the councils, as if they had not had enough experience with the council business in previous times. What prompted the "Swarajists" to this action has always remained unintelligible to me. Did they really believe that they could conquer the English bureaucracy of India through speeches in the council chambers, or frighten them into submission through their obstructionist terrors? If they did, it was a typical case of the triumph of hope over experience. If ever anyone made the English rulers of the country quake in their shoes it was Gandhi. He did not do this by the politician's tricks. He who fights against the English nation with those weapons works against heavy odds, because the English are already past masters in the art of diplomacy. The bureaucrats were terrified by Gandhi because he used the weapon of passive resistance, which was native to himself and his countrymen but foreign to the British militarists. The rulers of the country were completely baffled by Gandhi's methods. They simply did not know what to do. If it had been an armed insurrection of a rebellious nation, they possessed enough military force to suppress it with success; but their best strategists failed when they had to encounter a mass of three hundred million disobeying and yet non-resisting people, who had risen in sudden revolt against their established authority at the bidding of a saintly leader.

Gandhi's non-violent non-coöperation still forms the creed of the Indian National Congress. The masses all over the country have been made conscious of the loss of their national dignity under the rule of the British; the blood of the martyrs at Jallianwalla Bagh has made the heart of India bleed; and it is hoped that before the present agitation in the country is slackened, India will have achieved its national freedom, and have become able once more to offer its contribution of art, beauty, and culture to the rest of the world.

Other outside influences besides the injustices of the British rule in the country, that have conspired together to strengthen the nationalist movement of India during the twentieth century, were the Japanese victory in the Russo-Japanese war, and the lowering of the white man's prestige in the minds of all Eastern nations during and after the World War. The crushing defeat of the Russian forces at the hands of the Eastern islanders during the Russo-Japanese war broke forever the spell of the invincibility of white man's arms against Eastern foes; and this incident gave a great impetus to the nationalistic movements in all countries of the East.

Again when during the World War native regiments from the different colonial possessions of the fighting powers were gathered in the battlefields of Europe to witness the "white man's holocaust," their respect for his supposed superior civilization disappeared. At the same time the World War weakened the potential powers of the imperialistic white nations, thereby increasing considerably the chances of success for the rebellious peoples in the East. The high-sounding sentiments of "Self-determination" for weaker nations, and "a world made safe for democracy" uttered by the allied statesmen, during the period of war, had, ever since the ending of the World War on Armistice Day, quickened the hopes not only of India but of other dependent nations as well to seek in every direction for the realization of the ideals expressed by these eloquent orators of the allies. What will the end be?

* * * * *

Since this was written some developments of a momentous character have taken place in the political situation of India, of which an appropriate notice may conveniently be taken here.

At the 1928 session of the Indian National Congress held at Calcutta a scheme of self-government, jointly prepared by all parties in India, was presented to the British Parliament for enaction into law. This scheme, known as the Nehru Report, was accompanied by an ultimatum to the effect, that if Dominion Status equivalent to that of other self-governing dominions of the Empire like Canada and South Africa was not granted to India by the British Parliament before the midnight of December 31st, 1929, the Indian National Congress would henceforth declare complete independence as its immediate goal. Since no satisfactory response was made to this ultimatum by the British Parliament within the prescribed time limit, the Indian National Congress at its annual session held at Lahore during the last week of 1929 committed itself to complete independence and a severance of all relations with the British Government. The Independence resolution of Mahatma Gandhi was carried by an overwhelming majority of 2,994 votes against only 6. January 26th, 1930, was chosen by the Indian National Congress as the day of Indian Independence. It was observed by all Indians, in India and abroad, amidst spectacular demonstrations, during which the national flag was hoisted with ceremony, and the Declaration of Independence read to the masses. Resolutions of approval were passed at nearly 750,000 meetings, and pledges of support given to the Indian National Congress under the leadership of Mahatma Gandhi, by the enthusiastic crowds, everywhere. At a later date the All-India Congress Committee consisting of 300 members transferred its authority to guide the policies of the Congress to a working committee of ten chosen leaders of the people, who in turn have expressed their implicit faith in the leadership of Mahatma Gandhi.

After all efforts at reconciliation with the British Government had failed, Mahatma Gandhi embarked on his campaign of Civil Disobedience on March 9th, 1930. On that day he left his home at Ahmedabad with a batch of 79 volunteers to reach Jalalpur, a village on the ocean shore and 150 miles distant, where he and his followers will start manufacturing salt in open defiance of the British Government's monopoly of salt manufacture in India. This will be symbolic of Gandhi's program of Civil Disobedience. On this historic journey Gandhi and his followers have been greeted with tremendous enthusiasm by the general populace, who have gathered in numbers of hundreds of thousands and lined Gandhi's march all along his journey.

The plan of Gandhi is very simple. He, with his batch of volunteers, will start manufacturing salt at Jalalpur. Since this involves the disobedience of the civil authority of the British Government, it will be compelled to arrest Gandhi and his followers. The volunteers in case of their arrest will be replaced by other batches of equal numbers. In this way the campaign will continue until one of the parties withdraws. The Government will either succeed in breaking up the power of Gandhi's followers or yield to the demands of nationalistic India. On the one hand Gandhi has openly defied the British Government to arrest him, and on the other hand he has strictly enjoined his followers to maintain a spirit of non-violence. In a recent statement to the press he declared that he was not afraid so much of the wrath of the British Government as of the mad fury of his own countrymen bursting forth into open violence.

Gandhi's march to Jalalpur has aroused universal enthusiasm all over the country. Huge demonstrations are taking place everywhere. Indication of the British Government's policy of repression has shown itself already in the arrest of Gandhi's chief lieutenant, Mr. Vallabhai Patel, and the mayor of Calcutta, Mr. Sen Gupta. The masses have so far maintained the spirit of non-violence. Gandhi has given to the British Government of India the choice between a peaceful settlement and violence. He has been able so far to hold his countrymen in a calm mood of peaceful agitation. If he is arrested and the Government starts repression with its customary display of violence, the revolution in India may take a different course. In such a case the responsibility will be all England's.

Printed by Libri Plureos GmbH in Hamburg,
Germany